HYPER
AUTOMATION

Foreword by
Garry Kasparov

TABLE OF CONTENTS

Foreword

Garry Kasparov

We are in a time of crisis, as a pandemic wreaks havoc on human health and the global economy. With all our focus on the perilous present, it can be difficult to look ahead. We can easily fall behind relying on tactical reactions, losing sight of our bigger goals. Strategic planning becomes even more valuable in a crisis—not only for escaping the current one, but for being better positioned for the next.

Often our instinct in a crisis is to go on the defensive, to become more conservative in the hopes of weathering the storm. There is nothing necessarily wrong with this impulse—as long as we are aware of it and refuse to be dominated by it.

If we concede reason to instinct, we forfeit the greatest survival mechanism of all, the ability to adapt. This isn't a chess insight, or business strategy; it's basic Darwinism. Natural selection rewards the characteristics that best suit the circumstances, gradually producing change and evolution. A crisis accelerates the process—or ends the line.

Humans and our technology are subject to similar pressures, but we don't have to wait for random mutations or generations of life and death to evolve. We can observe, analyze, experiment, and strategize. We can build new tools to meet the demands of the moment, whether it's a financial crisis, pandemic, or both.

This ability doesn't mean we will always use it correctly, or make the right moves to adapt in the best way. But we have the potential to do that and more—to come through the crisis and thrive by making the right decisions while others falter.

This cannot happen unless we establish the right conditions—or at the very least it will be much more difficult and painful to achieve. Deep preparation was my trademark when I was the world chess champion. There was no way to be prepared for everything, but I knew I could be better prepared than my opponents.

I also discovered that my preparation produced benefits even when it didn't go as planned, even when my opponent avoided it entirely. My readiness was cumulative, multifaceted, enabling me to adapt on the fly. It turned out that pieces of preparation designed for one scenario applied surprisingly well to other situations that seemed unrelated on the surface.

Adaptation and creating the preconditions for adaptation—that's the human way of evolution. It applies to individuals, corporations, and our entire society. When a crisis hits, those who possess the right combination of characteristics have the advantage, but those who can acquire those characteristics on demand will thrive in any situation.

Now we've arrived at the topic of my first conversations with Matt Calkins, the founder and CEO of Appian. It turned out we were both fascinated by the potential of using increasingly intelligent machines to maximize this ability to adapt. We both see artificial intelligence as a tool that makes us better prepared, better able to meet a crisis—if we use it wisely.

My interest in working with AI came the hard way: my chess matches against the supercomputer Deep Blue in 1996 and 1997. The machine's victory in the rematch was hailed as an achievement on par with the Wright Brothers' first flight and the moon landing. It was described as "The Brain's Last Stand" on the cover of *Newsweek*. No pressure!

Of course, my loss to a machine was still a human victory. Deep Blue was created by a talented team that spent years of research and work to create a machine that could beat the world champion at a game long considered a nexus of human intelligence.

After losing that final game, I went out to a nice dinner with friends and talked about politics. And what did Deep Blue do? What else could it do, other than play chess? Nothing, of course. It couldn't even celebrate because it didn't know it had won. All that work, all that capability and cutting-edge hardware and code, couldn't be redirected into other tasks in any amount of time. It couldn't learn and couldn't adapt. It climbed Mount Everest, but it was also a dead end.

My personal adaptation was a form of "if you can't beat'em, join'em." If human strategic thinking and understanding could be combined with machine speed and precision, might it not produce the best chess ever?

Instead of human versus machine, why not human *plus* machine? And so, Advanced Chess was born.

My idea was simple, if heretical. Grandmasters would face off, each with a computer by their side running the best chess software available. My brainchild saw the light of day in León, Spain, in June 1998. My opponent was one of the world's top players, Veselin Topalov of Bulgaria. Playing with computer assistance was a strange sensation, although by then I was quite used to using a machine to help me with analysis and preparation.

It turned out to be far from the best chess ever, although the result was instructive. I had crushed Topalov in a match of regular rapid chess a few weeks earlier, a 4-0 sweep. But in León, it was a 3-3 tie. The machine's ruthless accuracy had neutralized my advantage in calculating tactics. Topalov and I failed to use our time efficiently, unsure of when to consult our machine partners and for how long.

Advanced Chess could have ended there as a curiosity, but eventually it found its natural home on the internet. In 2005, a popular chess site hosted what it called a "freestyle" chess tournament in which anyone could compete in teams with other players or computers. Lured by the substantial prize money, several groups of strong Grandmasters working with several computers at the same time entered the competition. At first, the results seemed predictable. The teams of human plus machine dominated even the strongest computers.

The surprise came at the conclusion of the event. The winner was revealed to be not a Grandmaster using top-of-the-line hardware, but a pair of amateur American chess players using three regular PCs at the same time. Their skill at manipulating and "coaching" their machines to look very deeply into positions effectively counteracted the superior chess understanding of their Grandmaster opponents and the superior computational power of other participants.

This led to my formulation: Average human + average machine + *better process* was superior to a strong computer alone and, more remarkably, superior to a strong human + fast machine + *inferior process*. It was about then that I started to prefer AI as "augmented intelligence." It doesn't replace us, it enhances us, and allows us to adapt faster by adapting our tools faster than ever. The human mind is an unmatched analogy engine, able to apply experience and new information to new circumstances almost instantly. Machines can't do this themselves—not yet— but with our guidance, they can help feed our insatiable appetite for ever-greater agility.

Process is king, a multiplier that turns human plus machine into a transformative advantage. As Matt Calkins says in his Introduction to this book: it's all about bringing human and digital workers together, to unite them into a workflow that is far greater than the sum of its parts. That's what those American chess amateurs did to beat Grandmasters and supercomputers, and that's what every company must do today to survive, and thrive, against unexpected challenges.

I could pick out many of my own favorite parts from this book, such as John R. Rymer's essential explanation of low-code platforms, or Darren Blake's real-life example of how adaptable software tools save lives in a pandemic. But I'll let you read them all yourself without further delay. After all, as every author to follow explains, speed is of the essence!

Garry Kasparov was the world's top chess player for 20 years and writes and speaks frequently on decision-making and the human-machine relationship. He is the author of Deep Thinking: Where Machine Intelligence Ends and Human Creativity Begins.

Introduction

Matt Calkins, CEO of Appian

Even before the COVID-19 pandemic, big changes were underway in enterprise software.

Corporations had become deeply reliant on software applications to automate their essential behaviors. Those applications, in turn, were stubbornly hard to update or modify.

Software had become the spinal cord of a business. Every action and every signal that passed through the company was carried by software. Every new behavior required software to enable and regulate it. This made software the limiting factor on corporate growth and change.

As companies grew, they needed to create new applications. Demand for these applications rose exponentially, faster than the labor supply could grow, making "software developer" one of the world's best-paid professions. Budgets rose, but still every company had a long backlog of processes to build and suffered universally from software delays.

Change was slow; costs were high. The stage was set for a revolution.

* * *

In the case of a crisis, every business was going to be dangerously inflexible. A company could move no faster than software allowed, and if new processes were slow to encode, so also would corporate reaction times be slow.

It is a fact that a corporation before 2020 could change any of its core assets more quickly than it could change its software processes. It could replace its leadership team, rebrand with a new logo, or move to a new physical headquarters faster than it could rewrite the software on which the corporation's behavior depended. Not only did this create internal inefficiency, it also led customers to feel they were treated impersonally and robotically.

The "digital transformation" movement sought to use new technology to overcome this immobility and unresponsiveness. It was discussed much, but accomplished little, due to a general misunderstanding about the depth of the problem and the urgency of its solution. It would take an exogenous shock to truly focus attention.

* * *

COVID-19 set the spark for the next phase of the enterprise software revolution. In the pandemic, business realized that change was a matter of survival. Every corporate relationship depended on an agile response to the crisis: customers and regulators demanded new behaviors, while employees needed assurances of safety.

Most businesses were unable to quickly adapt to the new circumstances. Because they couldn't change their applications fast enough, they were unable to express their new plans in new behavior. For example, most relied on non-technical systems to return their employees to work, despite the obvious safety and privacy disadvantages.

Companies today need to be ready at all times to write an application on which their business might depend. The new mandate is for agility in all applications, especially the most important ones.

COVID marked a turning point in enterprise software, an event that forced businesses to find ways to change their applications faster. Even when such an event ends, the preference for speed remains. Speed is addictive. Once people experienced Google's sub-second search times, or Amazon Prime's 2-day delivery, they were unlikely to go back.

* * *

"Automation" means bringing human and digital workers together in the same workflow. (In an earlier era, "automation" meant replacing people with technology, but now it means complementing them with digital helpers.) Automation is a uniting technology, and it comes along at a perfect time. Today, digital workers (like Artificial Intelligence and Robotic Process Automation) are powerful enough to collaborate with people on real tasks. Today, workers are more separate than ever before, and more in need of being connected.

Automation has a self-evident value proposition: different types of workers have different strengths, so they'll be better in combination. RPA Bots are fast and inexpensive but cannot handle exceptions or change. AI is great at evaluation, recognition, translation, and giving advice; but generally cannot make the final decision. People are best at making decisions and talking to customers. Without a doubt, these different workers can complete jobs more efficiently as a team, together in a single workflow.

The pandemic has forced people to work remotely from each other and collaborate over a distance. The workflow has replaced the workroom, as a coordination technology. We've never needed smart workflows as much as we do now, nor the full range of automation technology that fills them.

*   *   *

Hyperautomation is automation at speed. It's a combination between technologies that allow faster application authorship (like low-code and no-code) and automation technologies that coordinate different worker types. Both are essential in the new decade. Businesses will want to deploy workers more efficiently, and they will want to invent new work patterns faster.

The world has changed. Tomorrow's enterprise will need agility, unification, speed, and collaboration. In a word, it will need *hyperautomation*.

HYPER AUTOMATION

From Big Boxes to Intelligence Everywhere: The Changing Face of Automation

Neil Ward-Dutton, IDC

A look at how the world of business automation has changed through the decades, and how new technology capabilities have created new business possibilities. This chapter examines how new technologies come together with low-code development to deliver hyperautomation.

ABOUT THE AUTHOR:

Neil Ward-Dutton is Vice President, AI and Intelligent Process Automation European Practices, at IDC. Prior to joining IDC, Neil was Founder and Research Director of MWD Advisors, a technology advisory firm focusing on digital technologies and their impacts on business. Neil is recognized as one of Europe's most experienced and high-profile technology industry analysts. He has regularly appeared on TV and in print media over his 20-year industry analyst career as well as authored more than 10 books on IT and business strategy.

From Flour Mills to PCs: 250 Years of Business-Automation History

The history of business automation goes back a lot further than you might think. In 1785, American inventor Oliver Evans built an automated, water-powered flour mill near Newport, Delaware. Using a variety of automated mechanisms, Evans' invention enabled the mill to operate with just one person rather than four. When it worked optimally, it also produced flour from grain more efficiently than a non-automated mill. In subsequent decades, the invention and refinement of control systems enabled even more automation, of all kinds of manufacturing processes, at greater scale.

Second World War-era military efforts, and later, NASA's spaceflight program through the 1960s and 1970s, fueled the next major wave of innovation in automation. The first computers started to be set to work in business administration settings, as well as in manufacturing processes and scientific environments. It was a British food company, Lyons, that operated the first business applications on an electronic computer, starting in 1951 with a custom-built system to calculate valuations, process payroll and assess inventory. Through the 1960s and 1970s, computers in business were principally used to automate the work of clerks in accounting, payroll, and other relatively simple administrative functions, at scale; automating "standalone" functions; and creating and managing simple (if large) sets of administrative records.

Through many subsequent inventions and refinements in business computing—the introduction of digital computers, time-sharing systems, mainframe systems, local-area networking (LAN) technology, PCs and so on—businesses continued to focus their automation efforts on distinct administrative procedures and processes, albeit at vastly increased levels of scale and variation. It was only with the emergence of Enterprise Resource Planning (ERP) as a business discipline, in the late 1980s, that IT systems were built and operated to integrate automated business functions at scale: from HR to finance and accounting, production planning, and so on.

From the first introduction of computers in business contexts to the mid-1990s, the story of how businesses introduced automation was one of centralized design and development, high cost, concentrated use of specialized talent, and long gestation periods (with their attendant risks.) Large-scale, complex IT delivery models could only be applied to the most gnarly business challenges or the most obviously profitable business opportunities. The resulting systems operated at scale by necessity and could typically only be changed at significant cost and risk.

It's tempting to fast-forward to the present day and highlight how modern business automation technology has changed the game. But, it's not that simple. We got a taste of what is now happening at scale today for a relatively brief period, from the early 1990s to the early 2000s.

Rapid Application Development in the Client-server Era

In the early 1990s, an explosion of invention in networking technologies, server and PC platforms (together with a major shift in technology spending, away from centralization to distributed spending led by business units and functions) created a huge wave of opportunity to make computing more accessible to a wider range of businesses. This explosion, however, also created a huge wave of complexity for any team wanting to build business software. At the same time, the mass-market availability of new Graphical User Interface (GUI) technology, popularized by Microsoft, was making a massive impact. Combined with the success of the company's partner-centered business strategy, the result was a fast-growing ecosystem of partners offering new, low-cost, PC-based productivity applications with mass-market appeal.

For the first time, software vendors offered development tools that took advantage of new GUI environments and point-and-click techniques. The result was an explosion of tools that relatively non-technical staff could use to create relatively simple business applications. With the hugely popular Microsoft Visual Basic (introduced in 1991), Access, Delphi and PowerBuilder, together with niche products like Dynasty, Forte, JAM, Progress and Uniface (and many more), teams of business analysts and self-taught programmers were able to participate in (and often develop) end—to-end—business applications using visual tools.

This included so-called Rapid Application Development (RAD) techniques, based around the notion of iterative development. Through the 1990s, business function teams (and software development firms contracted to them) built and deployed tens of thousands of relatively simple, team-focused business software applications.

Some of these tools still remain. And perhaps unsurprisingly, many of the applications they were used to create are also still in use in businesses worldwide. At the end of the 1990s, though, a new technology-platform shift happened that most of these vendors struggled to embrace: the shift to web-based applications, where development-platform activity consolidated around Java and Microsoft's .NET programing languages.

Digital Transformation: The Imperative that Drives the Story

Curiously, the productivity advances that many of the "first-wave" low-code application development tool vendors had made in terms of visual, model-based development—not only of user interfaces, but also of business logic, data definitions, and so on—were forgotten in the early 2000s. A new wave of developers flocked to new Java- and .NET-based tools that required more technical development skills in order to build a new wave of e-commerce websites and applications that the RAD tools of the time were poorly equipped to help with.

Today, though, the pendulum of demand very definitely has swung back from the early 2000s, when web-based application development was dominated by technical developers working with relatively low-level tools. There are many reasons for this swing, but perhaps the most impactful is today's digital transformation imperative, which exists for businesses large and small in every industry.

The internet-based platforms for application and data hosting that first became usable in the early 2000s have become commodities. Hyperscale public cloud platform providers have created an abundance of scalable computing, storage and network capacity for rent. This has allowed waves of new "born-digital" businesses to compete for market share with established businesses across multiple industries—from banking and retail, to telecoms, utilities and even manufacturing.

For established businesses, the response to new "born-digital" competitors has to be to find ways to leverage digital technologies—not only to implement more sophisticated online marketing and commerce capabilities on the "outside" of their organizations, but also to integrate, streamline and increase the agility and scalability of the core business processes and decisions that drive the "inside" of their organizations.

Of course, the same rental models for computing infrastructure (known as Infrastructure-as-a-service, or IaaS) and business software development platforms (known as Platform-as-a-service, or PaaS) that new born-digital industry disruptors have leveraged are also available to established businesses. It's the global movement to take advantage of these platforms—to digitize business activities inside organizations, as well as outside—that is driving the new automation and that this book is all about.

A New Wave of Agile Business Automation Demand

Most organizations starting their digital transformation journeys begin by aiming to reinvent customer experiences—aiming to match the kinds of omnichannel, immediate, easy-to-use, personalized, and transparent interfaces that born-digital competitors place at the heart of their strategies.

However, organizations quickly realize that only focusing on the "digital outside" is not enough. An end-to-end customer journey is not only delivered with excellence through a great personalized website or a compelling mobile app. If, for example, your customer onboarding process is still largely manual, or if your billing systems are a legacy hangover from when you could only send paper bills to customers, the end-to-end experience for customers as they use your products and services is still likely to be poor. It could be argued, indeed, that by implementing a beautiful web app or mobile app you have actually made things worse than if you'd made no changes at all: you've made "experience promises" to customers and prospects that the inner workings of your organizations are not equipped to deliver.

For many established organizations, matters are made more challenging by internal operations historically developed to serve needs that are almost diametrically opposed to the needs of modern customers. Modern customers have expectations such as seamless service availability, integration and simplicity. The operations of established businesses were developed and managed to drive efficiency and scale—very often meaning that operations are siloed, globally dispersed (to lowest-cost locations), and delivered through complex networks of specialist partners.

Delivering excellence in modern customer experiences relies on the consistent, fast, transparent and agile execution of a whole chain of business tasks and processes. This is what drives us towards digitization of these tasks and processes. Because every chain is only as strong as its weakest link, no link (task or process) can be ignored. Addressing this digitization requirement across a complex, often siloed, business operations landscape is challenging, and hard to tackle with "big IT" projects, which are just too slow, too expensive, and too rigid in their approaches.

Luckily, the infrastructure and platform commoditization we've already highlighted has also created new economic conditions and capabilities that organizations are leveraging to enable smaller, quicker, cheaper and more iterative business-automation projects. There are dozens of cloud-based business application development platforms now available that can be accessed through monthly subscriptions. Often, they offer tiered pricing schemes, so organizations can get started on automation projects—delivering new digital business processes and related application functionality—very quickly, and at low cost. This is one way organizations can now effectively address the kinds of "long tail" problems and opportunities with digitization that were never economical to address in previous decades.

Robotic Process Automation: A New Vector for Automation

While cloud-delivered, subscription-based business application development tools have seen a rapid rise in popularity, another approach to business automation has been having a fast-growing impact on "long tail" business automation requirements.

Robotic Process Automation (RPA) tools, which first emerged in the late 2000s, were initially implemented by IT outsourcing and business process outsourcing (BPO) service providers to help them transform the processes they were carrying out for clients. The aim was improving service-delivery quality as well as improving their own profit margins. Specifically, RPA tools were used to automate the often highly-repetitive tasks that service delivery personnel were carrying out manually.

Such processes and tasks revolved around the use of legacy systems for data entry, data manipulation, reporting, and so on. With clients unlikely to approve the potentially expensive, risky replacement of legacy systems, RPA tools were designed to automate the tasks by running "software robots" that would copy the mouse movements, clicks and keystrokes of human users. Soon, RPA tools also started to be used within enterprises themselves, particularly (but not exclusively) in shared services centers responsible for business support functions like finance and accounting, HR, procurement, and so on.

By promising to free data and functionality locked away in legacy systems and automate routine data-entry and administration tasks, RPA technology brings the potential to "upgrade" slow, expensive, error-prone, manually-driven operations to make them more fit-for-purpose in the context of a business shift towards always-on, transparent, agile digital service delivery. It also provides low-impact, low-risk ways to accelerate technology change programs, such as large application migrations.

RPA tools and cloud-based business application development platforms address the opportunities and challenges of business automation from different directions, and they're also highly complementary. For example, organizations are increasingly using the workflow application functionality provided in modern application development platforms to implement robust exception handling for RPA.

This provides a scalable, transparent, controlled and auditable mechanism by which an operation can ensure that when RPA Bots break, the work they have not completed is correctly finalized. And Bots do break, for example when the legacy systems they're working against change, or stop working unexpectedly. Organizations are also using workflow application functionality to digitize business processes and co-ordinate the process work that teams of people do. Increasingly, they are complementing this with RPA functionality to automate individual tasks where data needs to be entered or read from one or more legacy systems.

There is a third force shaping the new business automation toolkit, which takes us into the world of "Intelligent Automation." This is the ability to apply Artificial Intelligence tools and techniques to a number of types of work—either to automate highly structured tasks completely, or to augment more creative or expert tasks that people do, using intelligent recommendations or predictions.

The New World of AI: Work Automation + Augmentation

Everywhere you turn, there's discussion of Artificial Intelligence technologies: discussion about what's possible today, how fast the technologies are changing, and the opportunities and challenges associated with implementation. It should be no surprise that AI-based technologies have several roles to play in today's business automation landscape. Nevertheless, not all of these roles are equally obvious. Let's look at three of these roles in particular.

The most obvious application of AI-based technologies for business automation is enabling system interactions based on natural language and speech. The possibilities of using something like Amazon's Alexa, Google's Home or Microsoft's Cortana to provide instructions to systems, or to have systems read out information to us, are easy to understand.

Even without an audible voice, modern text-based chatbot frameworks make it relatively easy to build fairly sophisticated conversational interfaces for customer-facing marketing, sales, and support functions; as well as employee-facing service functions (such as HR, IT, procurement and so on). Where implemented well, chatbots can dramatically increase employee productivity and customer satisfaction, as well as decrease the service workloads of employees in dealing with relatively simple requests. This enables workers to spend more time helping people with more complicated challenges.

This first kind of application of AI in business automation is perhaps the most transformational because it signals a shift in how automated systems and people interact. From the earliest days of automation—all the way back to automated flour mills in the 18th Century—until very recently, the introduction of automation has only become successful at scale because humans have adapted their behaviors to the requirements of those automations.

In factories and warehouses that leverage automation, human workers and automated systems have very clearly demarcated boundaries around their roles and operations. To be sure, in many cases there are physical boundaries that prevent people from getting in the way of automation technology. In office environments, we have learned to work in ways that suit our computers: typing and moving mice with our hands, and looking at rectangular screens to find information.

Yes, GUIs have improved the ease-of-use of modern computer systems, but we're still dancing to a computer's tune. Modern AI technologies and techniques are starting to enable a new kind of collaboration between human workers and automated systems—enabling automated systems to adapt to the ways that humans want to work, rather than the other way around.

Beyond this first kind of application of AI, there are two more that have the potential to make significant impacts in the world of business automation. The second key impact area for AI is in document analysis and processing. As we've already discussed, it's common for organizations pursuing digital agendas to introduce new online applications and systems—very often delivered via both "traditional" websites and mobile apps—to enhance customers' experiences.

However, particularly in business-to-business commerce, many interactions (apart from marketing and some sales interactions) are still, for a variety of reasons, carried out by document exchange. What's more, the specifics of those document exchanges can vary widely. In some business-to-business environments, fax is still a widely-used document exchange medium. In many industries, contracts and customer correspondence of all kinds are sent on paper, scanned or exchanged as human-readable PDFs.

When it comes to high-volume transactional document exchange (for example, exchange of purchase orders, invoices, delivery notes, and so on) scanned paper forms or human-readable PDFs are still often the norm. It's not uncommon for large multinational firms to process tens of thousands of human-readable invoices and purchase orders every month.

Optical Character Recognition (OCR) technology has been in use for decades, but it has important limitations: it can be brittle (being very "finicky" about how documents are presented for automated reading), it can suffer from poor recognition rates, and it can be slow. With modern AI-based approaches, though, human-readable documents can be more quickly and accurately "cleaned up" for automated reading—even when the initial clarity of text and other target elements is poor.

These documents can be more readily and quickly recognized and categorized, and key information can be more quickly and accurately extracted. In addition, AI-powered machine-translation algorithms can translate between human languages with high accuracy. And natural language processing algorithms can quickly determine the nature of the content of a document (for example, identifying the key parties in a long contract document and flagging the clauses that diverge from a standard model contract).

The third key impact area for AI in business automation is in the creation of real-time predictions and recommendations. For some years, specialized data science teams have been able to use predictive analytics platforms to analyze large data sets in order to produce predictive models, with the aim of forecasting, for example, the primary factors that will cause customers to churn, or, perhaps, when an expensive item of machinery is likely to fail.

Until recently, computing costs meant that these models could only be created and updated relatively infrequently: by organizations and use cases that could pass high bars for business returns. The large hyperscale cloud platform providers are having a big impact here, though, by making large-scale AI-based predictive models much cheaper to build, and cheaper and easier to update frequently.

As a result, AI-driven predictive models are showing up in more places and can be executed in real time against individual work cases and contexts. Now it's possible for contact-center software to surface a real-time prediction of a customer's likelihood of accepting a given offer, in the moment they are talking to a contact-center agent. It's possible for potentially fraudulent transactions to be flagged in near real-time; and it's possible for workflows and decisions to be more risk-based— for example, only sending customer product-return request cases for management review when a predictive model flags the return request as likely to be fraudulent.

Coping with Skills Gaps: Low-Code Approaches Democratize Automation

Although the economics of computing have shifted hugely over the past two decades to enable broad-based digital business experimentation, not all crucial resources have become more available. Organizations have serious challenges when it comes to hiring and retaining people with in-demand technology skills.

The availability of skills has always lagged the availability of transformational technology. Even back in the days of the first automated mills, it was relatively easy to find sites on which to build mills. But finding the technical skills and labor to build them was much, much harder. For decades, the growth in automated milling was constrained by the lack of availability of technical expertise.

Taking a traditional approach to software development to create new digitally-powered business capabilities can be challenging for many organizations. Consequently, more and more organizations—particularly those in industries that cannot easily compete for expensive, rare, digital development talent—are turning to new "low-code" automation tools and approaches to bring back many of the same capabilities and techniques first seen in the RAD tools of the 1990s. But companies are recasting these tools for today's technology and business environments.

All low-code development technologies share one common characteristic: they provide visual design tools that enable users to specify aspects of software behavior without resorting to coding. They then either generate executable code from those visual designs, or they generate an intermediate language that represents those visual designs, and then interpret that intermediate language using a proprietary execution engine at runtime.

Using low-code tools to design and deliver business automation projects can speed up capability development dramatically. It can also do something else really powerful: it can enable cross-functional teams that bring together relatively scarce technical specialists, business subject-matter experts, analysts, and less technically experienced staff to collaborate on projects. This matters because business automation projects are not purely technical projects: they are business change projects that affect how people work. When it comes to business change projects, involving the people whose work will be changed early and often is a critical success factor.

It's important to note, moreover, that low-code approaches to development aren't only being promoted and used in business application and workflow development (although that's where the trend is perhaps most obvious). The power of low-code tooling is also fundamental to the current success of RPA tools—where developers can specify the behaviors of robots by either recording and capturing sequences of user actions, or by dragging and dropping action definitions onto a graphical design canvas.

What's more, even AI tools are adopting the low-code philosophy: the workbenches and platforms now offered by the three most high-profile hyperscale cloud platform providers (AWS, Google and Microsoft) all include "AutoML" tools that relatively inexperienced teams can use to design and manage certain categories of machine-learning systems with graphical tools.

Lower-level software development tools and platforms will continue to play important roles indefinitely. That's as true for enterprises in financial services, healthcare, utilities and retail (and more) as it is for the companies that deliver commercial software tools, platforms and cloud services. Low-code tools can't do everything; they work best within designed-in constraints with which their graphical tools have been optimized to help. There will always be edge cases where low-code approaches are a poor fit. That said, the advantages of low-code tools—both in terms of raw speed and supporting iterative work within cross-functional, multidisciplinary teams that can understand and influence business change—makes them a perfect fit for any organization seriously pursuing a digital agenda.

Automation + Intelligence + Low-Code: Scaling for Success

In this chapter, we've explained how the world of business automation has changed through the decades, shown how new technology capabilities have changed what's possible—and how very old constraints (talent!) remain in place. We've also highlighted how low-code tools are permeating the business automation landscape. The combination of these trends around automation, artificial intelligence, and low-code development is the heart of hyperautomation.

As you start to explore opportunities to apply these new automation tools and techniques, there's one more thing to consider: how should you set up your organization so that initial successes can really scale? As low-code approaches increasingly dominate, and as cloud-based subscription services become increasingly popular, access to tools and skills is not the constraint it once was. In fact, as business automation rises up corporate leadership agendas, it's much more of a challenge to manage how best to apply tools and skills to the right problems in the right ways.

Of course, it's important that you pick technology tools and platforms that scale: both in terms of supporting applications that can support hundreds or thousands of users and high processing volumes; and in terms of supporting the parallel development and maintenance of many, perhaps tens or even hundreds, of applications by many different teams.

However, the most important enabler of all comes down to answering one vital question: how can you best set your organization up so that many individual teams can address their own opportunities and challenges with their own projects, while ensuring that teams work in ways that reinforce each other, that they build off each other's work and learnings, and that their work meets key enterprise requirements around operational scale, security, quality, reliability and so on? In other words: how do you best balance between enabling freedom and flexibility on one hand, and maintaining control and governance on the other?

As we explained above, the fundamental promise of low-code approaches in today's context is all about maximizing participation in the process of automation design and development. Wider participation brings improved application quality at lower risk; enables businesspeople to drive features and requirements more in line with real needs; speeds delivery; and minimizes reliance on expensive specialist software developers. However, broadening participation can lead to chaos, unless you exercise some level of control over how teams proceed with development work.

Leading organizations typically create this balance of participation and control through a Center of Excellence (CoE) that straddles the boundary that so often exists between business and IT teams. If created and run effectively, a CoE can play a central role within your business automation operating model to:

- Provide best-practice guidance and/or training to individual projects, in a way that helps teams not only to use the technologies at hand to their best effect, in the right combination, to suit the needs of each particular use case; but also to use the technology in ways that serve the organization's wider goals and strategies.

- Provide implementation and administration services to project teams, where those teams need specialized resources that don't necessarily make sense to manage full-time (for example, relating to specialized topics like identity management, application integration, aspects of UI design, etc).

- Manage centralized platform licensing and upgrade management for project teams, to ensure the organization gets the best deal for its license spend with its vendor(s).

- Harvest Intellectual Property (IP) from successful projects, identify assets that have potential to add value in multiple projects, and work to make them reusable.

- Review and approve applications prior to "go-live" to ensure that relevant standards and good practices have been followed.

It's vital to realize that there is no "one size fits all" model for a CoE. Organizations with highly centralized operating models can get great value from an all-encompassing CoE that delivers all of the services above; in contrast, in a more federated operating environment, a CoE that focuses primarily on promoting good practice and training can be a better fit.

Whatever CoE model is right for your organization, though, it's crucial that you look beyond technology choice. Delivering intelligent automation at scale—delivering real transformation with low-code automation technologies—can only come from using good tools, in the context of an operating model that encourages a healthy balance of flexibility and control.

How to Turn Your Company into a Master of Digital Transformation

George Westerman, Massachusetts Institute of Technology

Digital transformation is about much more than technology capability. Leadership capability is essential to guide a business through dramatic organizational change. Vision, an ability to bridge the IT/business divide, and effective governance all must go hand-in-hand.

ABOUT THE AUTHOR:

Dr. George Westerman works at the intersection of executive leadership and technology strategy. He is a Senior Lecturer at the MIT Sloan School of Management and Principal Research Scientist for Workforce Learning at the MIT Jameel World Education Lab. Westerman has co-authored three award-winning books, including Leading Digital: Turning Technology Into Business Transformation *and* The Real Business of IT: How CIOs Create and Communicate Value. *His writing, teaching, and consulting focus on helping leaders make sense of complex transformational challenges created by technological and market innovations.*

Digital Transformation Isn't Really a Technology Challenge

In recent months, much of the world has moved swiftly to confront the coronavirus (COVID-19) pandemic, which has infected and killed millions of people across the globe. The outbreak was a flare alerting us to systemic problems in our ability to adapt to a fast-moving threat that has disrupted everything in the global economy.

Organizations around the world moved quickly to digitally-distanced work processes, such as telemedicine, digital learning and working from home. But, while many adopted digital methods quickly, few were in a position to do it very well. They used technology to connect people but not to change what they did.

Likewise, every large business—in one way or another—is responding to the existential threat of digital disruption. The problem is that very few are doing it well. Most are adopting digital technology. But few have the capability to drive real transformation.

The best companies, which we call "Digital Masters," do two things better than everyone else: They are better at putting digital technology into customer experience, operations and business models. And they are better at envisioning and driving organizational transformation over and over again. Of the two—digital capability and leadership capability—leadership is the most important. Perhaps now more than ever, digital transformation isn't about being a digital company. It's about being a better company because of digital.

Driving Change from the Top

The human side of the equation—the organizational and cultural aspects—are critical success factors in the digital transformation journey. In fast-moving, born-digital organizations, people are a source of continual innovation. This should be the case in every company, but it's not. In a world of Moore's Law, where technology capabilities improve exponentially, we need to remember what I call the First Law of Digital Transformation: technology changes quickly, but organizations change much more slowly. That law means digital transformation is more of a leadership challenge than a technology challenge.

In our research, we observed how strategic-minded, digital leaders focused on transformation more than technology adoption. They looked at digital transformation as a capability and not just a project. And they used the following three levers to get the most out of their digital transformation strategy:

1. Create a strong vision for how to be a different kind of company because digital makes it possible.

2. Engage employees to help them understand the vision and the role they can play in helping the company move forward.

3. Implement governance to ensure the organization is coordinating, sharing, and driving transformation in the right direction.

I liken this to driving a car on a journey. The Vision is your destination. Engagement is your gas pedal. Governance is your steering wheel. You need all three to get where you're going. Then, when you get there, you set a new destination and do it all again.

Start with a Vision

The vision is your destination. Sometimes it's perfectly clear and you want to get there right away. Other times it's more of a goal, but you'll fill in the details on each step of the journey. The vision shows how things should be and makes it legitimate to do things differently from the past. As you consider building a vision for the future, make it big enough to encompass real change—a powerful journey, not just a trip to the grocery store. Aim to make the vision clear enough to set direction, but open enough that everyone can help to fill in the details.

After all, leaders in large organizations don't actually do anything. Their job is to get others to do things. If they do it well, the company succeeds. If not, then the company finds a new leader. That's why vision is so important. If it's compelling for you and your employees, they'll help you make progress. They'll even help you fill in some details or suggest new ways to go. But if it's only compelling for shareholders or leaders, you can expect little help from the people who actually do the work in the company.

Company leaders at Rio Tinto, a $43 billion mining and metals company, had a vision to understand operations better than they ever did before. And so, they connected their far-flung mines to a central control center, giving company leaders better visibility into local mining activities. Then, the leaders revisited their vision to figure out what else they could do. They took a hard look at improving the dangerous, routine work being done by workers inside the mines. For example, miners were driving huge vehicles around the mines in potentially dangerous conditions. But today, many of these vehicles have been automated, which has transformed the environment for workers. Other changes, such as autonomous drilling machinery and driverless trains, soon came online. Company leaders also found better, safer work for miners to do and and made continual improvements from there. The result was a mine that was more efficient for shareholders and safer for workers. It started with a compelling vision. Next, they executed through engagement, governance, and just plain project management. Finally, they revisited the vision to see what else they could do with their transformed systems and processes. This is what leadership capability is all about. It's not rocket science, but it's often forgotten in the rush to adopt technology instead of driving transformation.

The Importance of Engaging Your Employees

As I said earlier, the First Law of Digital Transformation holds that technology changes quickly, but organizations change much more slowly. Yes, technology can be a useful tool. But overcoming the inertia of a large organization is a leadership challenge.

This brings us back to the people part of the equation. There's no denying that the convergence of Robotic Process Automation and Artificial Intelligence has made it increasingly possible for companies to do work without human involvement. But don't make the mistake of thinking that you can use automation to push your organization to replace human workers while constantly ratcheting up pressure on the workers who remain. This is a near-sighted strategy that could turn employment into a purely transactional relationship, which would have negative implications for workers and companies alike. Digital transformation needs a heart. And it needs to capture the hearts of employees.

Digital leaders create environments where technology augments the capabilities of human workers; where computers help employees to collaborate fluidly, make decisions scientifically, and manage better than they ever could without them. In the long run, companies that engage the hearts and minds of employees will outperform those that don't.

The companies we call Digital Masters help their employees see a good place for themselves in the future vision of the company. They engage in a regular discussion about where the company is going, and how it can get there. They not only tell employees to change but also enlist employees in deciding how to change or identify new ideas for the company. For example, DBS Bank, one of Singapore's largest financial institutions, engaged their workers in a vision of "Make Banking Joyful." Employees are closest to the customer, and they see most of the problems that the company creates for customers—long lines, difficult loan processes, etc. By asking employees to help make banking joyful, the company identified and implemented a major transformation that took it from worst to best of the top five banks in the country.

Governance Doesn't Have to Be a Dirty Word

Moving at the speed of digital matters, but operating fast without compromising governance is more important than ever. In the worst-case scenario, governance can be a dirty word—a synonym for bureaucracy. In contrast, good governance is lean and agile, not bureaucratic and slow.

Governance is the steering wheel—it's how you keep your organization moving in the right direction. You move a bit with each project or experiment. And then you adjust so that you keep moving in the right direction. You help the right efforts, kill the wrong ones, and plant seeds for more growth. But be careful, since governance can sometimes be seen as preventing problems rather enabling progress.

If done right, governance will provide the right levels of sharing and coordination across your digital efforts. It won't be about "you can't do that" but instead will be about "here's a better way." Yes, this may still mean committees and reviews and shared resources. But if done with the right mindset, you'll learn with each step, and each step can build on the next to create powerful change.

Digital Plus IT, Not One or the Other

As we interviewed heads of companies and large business units, what we heard over and over again is: "Digital is fast but our IT department is slow. So, the only way we'll be successful with digital transformation is to leave the IT people out of the room." Our research showed that this was a poor choice. Digital Masters found ways for IT and Business to collaborate on digital. Sometimes the IT people led digital transformation. Sometimes it was the other way around. But no matter who led, they found ways for digital and IT and business leaders to work closely together in driving transformation.

The point is, you can't be successful at digital transformation—beyond the occasional, isolated project—without having IT people in the room. Much of an organization's legacy knowledge and processes reside in IT. So, if you exclude IT from the process, you end up trying to compete with startups without using the full power and know-how of your entire organization.

But that calls for change on both sides. Business leaders need to engage IT people in their business discussions. And IT people have to become the types of people that business leaders want in the room. If your company leaders think the CIO is actually the "CI-No," then you need to make changes. And if your IT unit is slow and stodgy rather than fast and agile, more change is needed.

Agile is a good starting place if you do it correctly. It helps IT to be faster and more innovative. And it helps IT and business people to collaborate more closely on making solutions happen. This produces better products faster, and increases the understanding that IT and business people have for each other.

Additionally, it's essential for IT leaders to show value for money in the IT unit—to demonstrate that you're providing the right services at the right level of quality and the right price. If you can't show you do your part well, it'll be hard for others to depend on you for their needs. And if your legacy platform is a mass of spaghetti, take steps to improve the situation, either by cleaning it up or putting good wrappers on key functions. We say much more about this in our book *The Real Business of IT*, which many CIOs call a cookbook for turning IT from order taker to strategic partner.

Next, gain better understanding of the business. Not only business terms, but also what really matters to each executive. How does her part of the business work? What are her big challenges? What can you suggest that might help her run her business better or more profitably? Not all of your ideas will be accepted. But on those that are, be prepared to deliver quickly and well. By doing this repeatedly, you'll make your C-suite peers want to spend more time with you.

CIOs can lead digital transformation, but often another leader does. I've seen many cases where that becomes a reason for conflict, with each trying to undermine the other. When that happens, the CIO rarely comes out on top. Far better to get clear on roles and to coordinate closely, so that you can improve the company together as a team.

A Better Strategy, Enabled by Digital

Schindler Elevator doesn't just sell elevators and escalators. It sells urban mobility. An integrated suite of devices adjusts for traffic levels and other conditions minute-by-minute. The company aims to do maintenance based on the actual condition of each machine rather than a fixed schedule. For Schindler, that's a whole different way of doing business —turning their products into services.

Asian Paints, transformed from selling paint differently in 13 regions of India to a unified supplier of paint, painting services, and building services in almost two dozen countries. Asian Paints is a better company because of digital. But digital technology was not the answer. Repeated transformation, enabled by digital, was. In other words, your company doesn't need a digital strategy. It needs a better strategy, enabled by digital.

There's no denying the term *digital transformation* has been over-hyped. Google it and you'll get millions of results. It's been that way for over a decade. Keep in mind that technology has always enabled change, and this is why digital transformation will be relevant now and in the future. But don't get caught up in "magical thinking" about the powers of digital transformation. Don't believe the marketing hype that: "If I buy this shiny new technology and plug it into my organization, it's going to make us better." It won't.

It's way more important to understand how your organization works. You don't become a Digital Master by just buying technology and plugging it in. There's an awful lot of organizational change that has to happen first. Simply investing in Artificial Intelligence and automation is not going to do that. Better to figure out how to leverage these technologies to do business differently.

E-commerce is not about the internet. It's about selling differently. In the same way, analytics is not about databases and algorithms; it's about understanding customers better, optimizing maintenance processes, or helping doctors diagnose cancer more accurately. And The Internet of

Things is not just about identifying objects with RFID tags; it's about radically synchronizing operations or changing business models.

Get Digital Enough: Three Keys to Building a Digital Culture

There's a famous quote by Charles Darwin that says: "It's not the strongest of the species that survives, nor the most intelligent... It is the one that is most adaptable to change." There's a parallel in business: if you don't know what to change or how to change, you won't survive.

It can be tempting to emulate the cultures of digital darlings such as Amazon, Google, Netflix, or your favorite digital startup. They are fast, innovative, and expert at using technology to drive opportunity.

But traditional companies can't copy everything the digital-born stars do. Most companies can't hire, incent, or fire the way these fast-moving businesses can. Instead of websites and apps that can change quickly, most companies build physical objects that don't change once built. And they often have to follow regulations that startups sometimes dodge while they are small. That doesn't mean traditional companies should give up; they should just be smart about the digital culture "secrets" they try to adopt.

A better alternative is to get digital enough. This means being faster and more innovative while following regulations and giving your people a decent work-life balance. I wrote about this strategy this year in an article called "*Building Digital Culture in Traditional Organizations.*" Basically, there are three keys to getting digital enough:

1. Become more Agile—more experimental and self-organizing the way that digital companies do. In other words, do Agile. Don't just say you're doing it.

2. Keep the practices that foster integrity and employee stability. You can still be innovative, and your workers will reward you with loyalty and great ideas.

3. Finally, rethink what it means to manage to numbers and customer needs. The best companies are tracking customer interaction data every minute, every day, not every quarter. Turns out the best companies are also constantly experimenting to see what customers want rather than asking customers to tell them what they want.

Change Continues to Accelerate

It's like 1999 all over again. In retrospect, the run-up to Y2K was a catalyst for change, and the internet was an exciting way to rethink how we did business. Now COVID-19 is a catalyst for more change. It made us realize that things we once felt companies and customers would never accept—working from home, telemedicine, etc.,—can work very well. We're more able to innovate today because cloud, containers, mobile, sensors, machine learning, and other technologies are becoming ubiquitous, interoperable, and increasingly capable. Along with that, innovations in software development, such as Agile, DevOps, and low-code, are helping organizations be faster and more innovative in applying technology to make transformation happen.

Looking ahead, if you're trying to anticipate what to expect over the next five to 10 years, consider that the pace of transformational change will continue to accelerate in the digital economy. Every organization will need to get much better at being Agile, being innovative, and leveraging existing assets for new opportunities. There's a growing sense of urgency for every organization to build the capability required to transform over and over again—and make that a fundamental part of their core culture. In other words, for every company, becoming a Digital Master is an existential challenge.

The bad news is that there are many ways to fail at digital transformation. Overcommitting to the wrong strategy. Focusing too much on technology as a solution. Trying to copy the culture of digital leaders without considering how the practices fit your world. Expecting IT leaders (or digital leaders) to do it totally on their own. Investing too heavily when the market is not yet ready. And there are dozens more.

The good news is that you can do something about this. For starters, focus on building leadership capabilities—for vision, transformation, and culture—not just technology skills and tools. Aim to understand the business better, so you can help your C-suite peers find new and better ways to solve business problems and meet customer expectations. But the most important capability for any organization to invest in right now is the ability to innovate quickly. In the age of digital transformation, this should be a core part of every company's culture.

Survival of the Quickest: How to Hack a Pandemic with Intelligent Automation

Lakshmi N, Tata Consultancy Services

How is your organization preparing for the massive volatility and uncertainty of the global COVID-19 recession? You can stack the odds in your favor by augmenting human capabilities with intelligent automation, getting into an Agile mindset, and finding and encouraging diversity of thought.

ABOUT THE AUTHOR:

Muthulakshmi (Lakshmi) N is Global Head of Intelligent Process Automation and AI at Tata Consultancy Services (TCS), India's largest information services company. She has more than 18 years of experience in managing large transformation programs for Fortune 100 Clients in the U.S. and Europe. Lakshmi has also led and played a crucial role in a variety of strategic initiatives including TCS's MFDM™ (Machine First Delivery Model) which reimagined how digital transformation delivers exponential value.

Nobody knows for sure what the post-COVID-19 world will look like. But you can certainly bet it's going to be different. The pandemic has already pummeled the global economy and exposed weaknesses in supply chains and vintage software systems. At the same time, it has accelerated automated delivery of goods and services, and autonomous customer interactions. It has also forced companies once skeptical of work-from-home culture to embrace it more than ever before.

And, yet, for many executives, a major roadblock to scaling automation is the misconception that aggressive, holistic automation will result in widespread job loss. This dystopian view fails to imagine the new types of jobs that will come from automation liberating employees from routine work that can be done faster, better, and less expensively by Artificial Intelligence (AI).

As the global head of the intelligent process automation practice at Tata Consultancy Services (TCS)—a $22 billion IT services company with more than 443,000 employees worldwide—I know firsthand that intelligent automation is not just about replacing human workers with digital labor. But, it's also about delivering business value with Artificial Intelligence and analytics in every aspect of the enterprise.

To remain relevant in the age of COVID, businesses will need quicker, smarter, and more flexible digital capabilities. This seems pretty obvious.

But there were enterprises—despite being aware of the drastic impact of the pandemic—that were still ill prepared to adapt and evolve. The question is, how is your organization preparing for the post-COVID world? Do you have the Robotic Process Automation, Business Process Management, AI, and analytics capabilities you need to quickly adapt to face the massive volatility and uncertainty of the global COVID recession?

It seems that everything turns out better when we're prepared. And during a pandemic, being prepared costs much less than being caught unprepared. It's important that we should work overtime to compete in an environment of volatility and uncertainty that will last a while. But you can stack the odds in your favor if you leverage automation to augment the capabilities of your workforce and drive long-term value for your customers. At TCS, we call this empowering the human workforce by giving them the first right of refusal to any technology that augments their capabilities.

Giving First Right of Refusal to Technology

There are so many things we can say about automation. We've built a digital economy on it. And while we can be cautious about adopting automation, that would be a mistake. Nevermind the hype about automation killing jobs. Strategically speaking, automation is not about replacing the human workforce. It's about using digital technology to drive long-term business value in every aspect of the enterprise.

The difficulty of scaling automation is fundamentally an organizational challenge as much as a technology challenge. So, at TCS, we've adopted a Machine First mindset that redefines the traditional approach to enterprise automation. It doesn't necessarily view automation as a headcount reducer. Rather, it's a digital transformation strategy based on giving the first right of refusal to technology.

So, what exactly does it mean to give technology the first right of refusal? It means looking at every business activity performed manually in your organization and asking: "Can a machine do it better?" This is a transformative mindset that focuses on what customers and businesses really value.

It's the best way to get the most business value out of cloud computing, Artificial Intelligence, and analytics in every aspect of the enterprise. So, for example, even if you're talking about building and deploying an application to transform an HR or Marketing organization for a client, every human worker should be empowered to give the first right of refusal to any technology that would augment their own capabilities.

With the astonishing evolution of AI, automation is no longer just an interloper. It has become an integral part of our lives. When you tune into Netflix, if you don't like it, if it doesn't meet your expectations, you'll just switch to another service. Future generations of digital consumers will be even more demanding than that.

Low-Code: Elevating the Automation Game

I've been with TCS for almost 15 years now. But my journey with intelligent automation began about two years ago, before COVID, social distancing and lockdowns became a reality. The pandemic hit us hard in mid-March, which prompted many customers to put long-term strategic initiatives on hold. The opposite was true of demand for intelligent automation. It offered clients a better alternative to the unprecedented disruption the pandemic created. Our most successful clients understood that setting up the right automation foundation would give them a strategic advantage by allowing them to adapt faster than their competitors to the ongoing volatility of the post-COVID economy.

Speaking of adapting to COVID, before the outbreak, only 20% of TCS's employees worked from home. Today, nearly 90% work remotely and mostly because of the pandemic. How remarkable is that—empowering more than 400,000 employees to work from home in just a matter of days? We were able to do that because of the strong foundation of intelligent automation and Agile methodology we already had in place.

Beyond Automating Stuff

Yes, low-code offers unsurpassed efficiency in building applications. But beyond that, it also takes the complexity out of combining technologies, orchestrating processes and optimizing human-machine interactions. This changes the automation game completely. Let's say, for example, you want to automate the lending process of a bank. For starters, there will be digital screen entries, paper documents, and data collected from forms, and a system for approving loans. This is where low-code comes in. It gives you the capability to quickly develop applications that connect and automate across systems, people, processes, and data to take friction out of the customer and remote employee experience. As the global economy grinds to a halt amid COVID lockdowns and massive job loss, experts are urging businesses to get more aggressive about transitioning to a more automated economy.

"... Simply put, you need a foundation for rapid process automation now. If your organization is already using a low-code, Digital Process Automation, or Workflow management platform, apply it actively to automate all processes that can be automated."

So says Forrester Research.

With the devastation of the pandemic, the U.S. economy could shrink by a whopping 5.6% in 2020 and end the year with a double-digit unemployment rate and millions of people forced into isolation. But COVID won't just shut down the economy. Critically, it will continue to expose weak spots in the vintage technology that many organizations are running on.

IBM recently reported that:

- 92 of the top 100 banks use mainframe technology to provide customer service.

- 70% of enterprise data resides on a mainframe.

- 71% of Fortune 500 use a mainframe.

- 23 of the world's top 25 retailers use the mainframe for customer service.

- All Top 10 insurers use the cloud on the mainframe.

But the pandemic will end one day. The masks will come off and stay-at-home orders will end. In the meantime, though, how can you get the flywheel spinning on business recovery? And if you're eager to do that, how do you combine digital and human labor to quickly respond to the coronavirus crisis and rally your business after the pandemic subsides? Automation is an essential part of the equation to do that. But we must also get serious about advancing the next generation of women leaders to take us to higher levels of innovation and economic growth. The thing is, not to make the mistake of thinking that gender bias is just a woman problem. It's a bug in the system that affects us all. Studies show, for example, that prioritizing career advancement and pay parity for women would add a staggering $12 trillion to the global economy by 2025.

Which also calls for us to seriously consider how the exponential growth of intelligent automation and AI will affect gender equity in the workplace. It also means rethinking the connections between digital transformation and gender parity. What the strategies should be to achieve it, what the policies around it should be, and what kind of pragmatic action needs to be taken now.

But change is hard. And, so, we see progress for women in business continuing to move at glacial speed. Female senior execs at Fortune 500 companies are mostly invisible, "hidden figures" so to speak. Too few women get the corner office. At a macro level, just one in five C-suite execs are women. And only one in twenty-five is a woman of color. Females make up about 25% of the tech workforce but hold only 5% of the leadership positions. Gender and racial exclusion is toxic to innovation. Much better to have more women and people of color in power positions to keep things moving forward. India's Debjani Ghosh, President, of the National Association of Software & Services Companies said it best:

"We are having real conversations now about getting more women into every level of our organizations and onto boards, and that's a good thing. But we need to get beyond conversations. We need to get to the point where every CEO believes that if we don't do this, we will lose relevance and customers, and realize that competitors who are embracing diversity will win."

Evangelizing Enterprise-Wide Automation

Over the years, I've learned that federated organizations struggle to scale automation. Individual units within a complex organization tend to be driven by different priorities, which can get in the way of evangelizing an enterprise-wide automation strategy. Consequently, automation in the enterprise tends to happen in silos where it's mostly driven by efficiency. I've also seen situations where too many people in a large company didn't understand the technology being evangelized or the business value it represented.

So, how do you fix the disconnect? You do it by starting with a platform for growth, a low-code platform that allows you to quickly combine and orchestrate different technologies. From a governance standpoint, it means putting policies in place to safeguard data access, and security. It also means educating internal teams to understand how the organization, customers and end-users benefit from intelligent automation.

Digital Inclusivity, A Critical Success Factor

I recently talked to a woman thought leader about the problem of digital exclusion. We talked about the business case for attracting more women into technology jobs, and about the urgent need to advance the careers of women and people of color already working in the industry. Focusing on diversity matters because we're operating in an increasingly diverse world where demographic shifts have fragmented the market more than ever before. Modern consumers are more intergenerational, a mixture of Baby Boomers, Millennials, Gen Xers and more.

In the next decade, understanding diversity trends will be key to cashing in on emerging opportunities that might otherwise get overlooked. Due diligence helps us see the unseen. In the United States, for example, millennials—who now represent 30% of the population—are the most diverse generation in U.S. history according to Deloitte. Ethnic and racial minorities make up roughly 44% of the cohort. But beyond the digits, a critical part of the inclusion narrative is debunking the myth that women don't want to be leaders. The inherent leadership skills that women bring to the table are really needed in the post-COVID economy—skills like collaboration, being open to learning and building relationships. We also need more women in tech jobs. But we don't need to sacrifice one for the other. There's room for both.

Some companies care about the appearance of diversity—not figuring out how to turn inclusion into business outcomes. But diversity and inclusion aren't just about checking a box on a diversity checklist. In a diverse world, it's difficult to be a customer-focused business if you don't build technology that works for everyone. And it's hard to do that in an organization that doesn't value gender parity and diversity of thinking as a business strategy. When you ignore the strategic value of being inclusive, you diminish your ability to be a market leader in terms of productivity and profitability.

On the other hand, if you care enough to think strategically about inclusion, it's hard to ignore the following five connections between diversity, performance, and profitability, based on recent research from McKinsey:

1. Companies with the most ethnically and culturally diverse boards worldwide are 43% more likely to experience higher profits

2. Companies in the top-quartile for gender diversity on executive teams were over 20% more likely to outperform competitors on profitability and value creation

3. The best performing companies on both profitability and diversity had more women in revenue-generating roles on their executive teams

4. Companies that led on executive team diversity were 33% more likely to have industry-leading profitability

5. Brands in the bottom quartile for gender and ethnic/cultural diversity were 29% less likely to achieve above-average profitability

Across the globe, the pace of digital transformation is accelerating. The coronavirus pandemic has forced us to invest in automation to get through the lockdowns. It has forced us to adapt our business models to meet increasingly diverse and demanding customer expectations. The evolution of technology is continuing to blur the boundaries of the physical and digital worlds, redefine traditional borders between industries, and fundamentally change how we live, work, and interact with machines. I also see a future of contactless customer experience, created by a combination of the Internet of Things, AI, and intelligent automation that will create a brave new world of magical customer experience.

End of the day, it all boils down to the fact that the most successful organizations will recognize the secret to success as leveraging diversity and inclusion. But it's hard to do that without women and people of color. The same is true of digital transformation. It's entirely possible to factor the diversity of a target market into the application we create to serve it. But businesses must get better at that. It will take an enormous amount of effort and persistence to get there. But as I look to the future of automation, to the next decade and beyond, I'm optimistic that the arc of digital transformation will bend toward inclusion.

From Hurricanes to COVID-19 and Beyond: How Low-Code Helps our University

Sidney Fernandes & Alice Wei, University of South Florida

Seasoned low-code practitioners discuss automating and mobilizing a major university for student success, operational efficiency, and cost-avoidance, and low-code's vital role in helping the university communicate and coordinate during times of crisis.

ABOUT THE AUTHORS:

Sidney Fernandes is the Vice President/CIO for Information Technology for the University of South Florida. Sidney fosters a culture focused on transformation, influence, collaboration, strategy and vision. He and his leadership team have evolved the USF IT work environment to have an Agile methodology mindset, be client centered, and reflect core values of respect, focus, openness, commitment, courage, and a growth mindset.

Alice Wei is the University of South Florida's Senior Director of Digital Innovations.

By the summer of 2017, we had already been using low-code technology at the University of South Florida for a few years. We had experience, and we had successes under our belts. So, when Hurricane Irma was predicted to hit—and to hit very hard—that summer, using low-code was naturally part of our response.

We needed to create some solutions very quickly. In the days immediately following Irma, we needed to connect with our community of students, faculty, and staff. Opening lines of communication between constituents became a top priority. We needed to know how people were doing, and answer questions with real-time updates.

Using low-code, we were able to get an app up and running in a matter of hours. Literally, overnight. We started at 3 or 4pm and by 8am the next morning we had automations in place to connect our constituents and streamline information flow and processes. We could proactively collect information and run analytics about what people were calling about, and how we could direct and respond to those questions.

We were able to move that fast because, as established low-code developers, we already had building blocks in place. We had authentication, we had student records, faculty records, and more, which we were able to stitch together very quickly. This architectural library of components and integrations is why low-code actually gets faster the more you use it.

In the end—and thankfully—Irma didn't inflict as much damage on our region as predicted. Our low-code response to the hurricane, however, did provide experience that would come back to bear in the COVID-19 pandemic.

With our large, 50,000-plus student community, we've seen how low-code systems provide agility, flexibility and communication pathways to centralize accurate information about our people, where they are, and what they might need. Connecting our whole community in a timely fashion is key to coordinating our organization during crises.

In the wake of COVID-19 and the myriad challenges it presents, we again looked to low-code to coordinate the safe return of our students, faculty, and staff members to our three campuses across the state of Florida. Institutions of higher learning like ours have organizationally-unique and campus-specific needs. Because we—like all other colleges and universities—now find ourselves in an ever-evolving environment with frequently changing requirements, we needed to embrace a flexible solution that would allow us to quickly make changes.

From the outset, we knew how important it was to get students, faculty and staff back on campus but in a way that protects the health and safety of all concerned. Our COVID-19 Task Force—launched in March 2020 with folks from all aspects of the university—scoped out a dynamic, flexible plan designed to make it as easy as possible to maintain distance, wear masks and, most importantly, self-report possible COVID-related symptoms. Time was critical. So, we needed an out-of-the-box platform solution: a solution that could provide accurate, timely data to be shared with leaders and decision-makers at USF.

The result was our CampusPass app, which provides vital help with the challenges of tracking students and following cases based on return-to-campus surveys. Through low-code development, we were able to rapidly stand up this incident-management application to support the university's goal of keeping track of all cases, including contact tracing —with speedy personal communication and sustained compliance with all state and federal regulations.

We knew we had to strike a fine balance: leveraging state-of-the art Platform as a Service (PaaS) technology to coordinate the complex return-to-campus process and manage on-going health and safety concerns, while, at the same time, protecting sensitive health information. At USF, we prioritize data security for healthcare data, so our solution runs on a HIPPA-compliant and HITRUST certified secure cloud. When you are a CIO, the first thing you think about is the protection of data. That's why a platform approach is critical.

In just a month or two, we were able to centralize and automate time-sensitive data in an integrated, holistic solution to support on-campus health and safety. But successfully managing crises like hurricanes and a COVID-19 response is only one part of a broader theme we embrace at USF: digital transformation in the campus setting.

Digital transformation—whether in an enterprise setting or on a university campus—is hard work. For university chief information officers and campus IT execs like ourselves, the question is: What automation tools are available to help get our students, faculty and staff to the best possible outcomes in their respective pursuits in the academic world?

Our role at USF is to try to make sure our students and faculty have the best overall experience while they are at the university. We've even begun to talk about students being life-long students—students "forever" in terms of learning things throughout their life at USF. We're focused on their experience before joining USF. Their onboarding experience when they first come here, which can be a confusing time. Then, later while they are enrolled as undergraduates and graduate students. Finally, we focus on students when they become alumni.

Student success remains front and center in our list of priorities. For our faculty, we're focused on making sure they get to do what faculty do best: teach our students to do research, and, in the case of our medical and health faculty, serve our patients as well. Simply put, our long-term focus has been: How can we create digital experiences for students and faculty that make their lives easier and simplify the complex bureaucracy that can exist at a university?

The Journey to Low Code

In retrospect, the background to our pivot to low-code has several key milestones.

First, we realized that the way we did work here—say some five to ten years ago (way before all the digital transformation buzz!)—was just not going to succeed for a large university setting. What universities traditionally do, as was the case at USF, is to hire a bunch of highly skilled developers—in our case we were a Cold Fusion, Python-shop—to create point-solutions for whatever folks were screaming about. We had 16 programmers and about 150 built-from-scratch, custom-code apps… and we had tons of technical debt that we were never going to get to.

It was a tough situation, to say the least. We had a backlog of some 100-odd projects that our clients were still waiting on. And there was no capacity for new development. There was just constant conflict between "Do we fix up this old application or build a new one?" That said, our clients didn't want us to waste their investments on fixing the old stuff. So, the old apps just kept getting worse and worse. At the same time, we desperately wanted to develop some new fun, more complex solutions for student success. This included, for example, call-to-action-type functions on the web page—one of which would help students select a profession based on their major. So, we went looking for tools in the market and spoke with Gartner and others extensively.

That's when we learned about the emergence of low-code technology, and how it could provide us with tools to handle the baseline low-hanging-fruit applications (basic forms and more forms), while at the same time free up our programmers to create some of the more fun and complex student-facing solutions we wanted. We needed a robust, scalable platform that could improve our student experience while driving operational efficiencies for faculty and administration (HR, travel, faculty tenure, promotion and the like). Our vision was: a lot of things our programmers built should be seen as components that are reusable.

For example, if you're building a log-in screen, it's the same log-in screen for every portal and app you've built. Why should you have to rebuild it again and again; why should you have to maintain the code for each use case and go into each individual application and update it? That's how we had rolled for years. But we decided to pivot and look for a tool that would allow for a library of reusable pieces, and also enable us to develop applications faster.

Ideally, these reusable pieces would be like Lego parts that we could take apart and rebuild at very rapid speed to create an optimal 21st Century teaching and learning environment. We found this capability in an enterprise-grade, low-code development platform that's quickly able to deliver innovative applications which eliminate waste, improve performance and enhance the end-user digital experience for students.

Where We are Today

At USF, where low-code is now very much part of our digital DNA, our information technology division spans the following technology services and support offerings:

- **Teaching and Learning**: technology in the classroom, smart computing labs.

- **Administrative**: management and integration of student and admin systems.

- **Communication**: online community and collaboration.

- **Analytics and Reporting**: interactive dashboards, business intelligence.

- **Mobile and Web Solutions**: dynamic, secure web and mobile solutions.

- **Consulting**: research, visualization, modeling, project management.

- **Cybersecurity**: risk management, data protection, encryption, monitoring.

To meet the fast-moving and ever-changing needs of multiple business units, we couldn't afford to rely on our "old" system, because it could take months or years to push through an upgrade for a critical solution or create an entirely new set of applications. In contrast, our needs are now being met in literally weeks or months with an agile, enterprise-grade, scalable low-code app development platform. Instead of being forced to spend $10 million to $20 million for massive overhauls of existing student-information-systems, as some universities currently face, we only spend in the thousands of dollars to get time-critical upgrades and new app development pushed through for our clients.

That's because we need fewer of the very highly skilled programmers typically required to execute on our mission within our modern digital ecosystem, which includes a full range of technologies such as: ERP, BPM, RPA, low-code and related agile app dev methodologies.

Why do universities need to use low-code as part of the strategic equation going forward? Because ERPs at universities are not able to do everything universities need to get done. With the traditional framework of disparate teams of developers spread throughout the university and with so many niche applications, it takes too long for central IT to respond with effective student-success and automation/process solutions. What we've found at USF is that we can now code at the speed of the clients or sometimes faster, because we have a low-code platform that can do what ERPs are unable to do.

What's more, ERPs in education tend to be more clunky. The people that use them on a daily basis are okay with that. But people unfamiliar with ERPs—like students and faculty and certain staff—often find them difficult to drive, so to speak. So in a lot of cases, at various universities, you have people thinking about a complete ERP reimplementation. But at USF, we decided to integrate our existing ERP with a low-code platform that would allow faculty and students to quickly interact with the ERP in a modern environment—including both desktop and mobile—at the speed of the client.

Here's why university CIOs and their respective teams should consider adopting best-of-breed enterprise-grade low-code:

- It creates solutions at the speed of the client

- It creates enterprise-grade solutions for large-scale implementations better than ERPs

Universities, simply put, have an unlimited demand for automation of processes. They traditionally have lots and lots of old-school, paper-based processes that are crying out for automation. Students may be required to submit forms for everything—for classes, for health services, for change of advisor, and on and on. Consequently, students must also be able to complete these interactions in an automated manner. Turns out today's students—yes, these Generation Z students in particular—expect to engage with mobile apps and get information quickly. So, you want to be able to build solutions for this generation that has essentially grown up as digital natives.

One of the low-code initiatives we are most proud of here at USF are our student-success, student-lifecycle case-management solutions. These applications unite support personnel—including academic advisors, career counselors, financial advisors, residential life coordinators and more—in a single web and mobile application to efficiently assist an individual student's progress to graduation. It's all about proactively providing care for at-risk students when they need it, whether they know they need it or not.

We gather all student data on a single platform. This allows for anyone who wants to help the student to see the same data, update the information, and reach out to a student as well. The solution incorporates records data-management, collaboration and predictive analytics capabilities (including AI) to provide insightful and time-sensitive information on individual students. We believe this low-code derived app has helped improve USF's graduation rate from levels around 50% to more than 70% in recent years. Technology has played a role in the improved graduation and retention rates at USF. But it's impossible to know to what extent. That said, we are moving rapidly to make this digital "triage" available across all of our geographically distinct campuses.

When it comes to driving future technology investments at USF, our vision is focused on supporting the handful of strategic priorities that the university has identified: student success, promoting research and innovation, and overall improvement of the customer experience. We believe the CIO role here—and similarly at other major institutions of higher learning across the nation—is rapidly evolving.

Truth is, expectations of the CIO are quickly changing from merely being a respected go-to person for identifying and deploying hardware and software solutions to being a trusted partner of the business unit when it comes to developing solutions in near real-time. In other words, the modern CIO is expected to be a broker of technology solutions—increasingly mobile-first applications—across the campus. Based on that strategic shift, it's also incumbent on the CIO to put in place certain key performance indicators (KPIs) and other metrics to ensure all IT projects are aligned to business goals.

ROI of Low-Code on Campus

In addition to the many tangible benefits in terms of student success and operational efficiencies, low code implementation has a very significant ROI when it comes to cost-avoidance. Today, colleges, universities and all types of institutions of higher learning across the nation face a major debate when it comes to upgrading their legacy systems of record: few institutions, to be sure, are actively thinking of jettisoning their entire, generations-old ERP systems.

These student-information-systems and related embeds are not going anywhere. The problem is that they are overburdened with layer upon layer of modifications and so-called bolt-ons that keep the overall systems from living up to expectations. Technical debt abounds. At USF, we've found that by adopting low-code, we are able to gain more access to—and more functionality from—core legacy systems. And this at a fraction of the costs of a major overhaul or systemic upgrade to the standing ERP. Why invest tens of millions of dollars, as many universities are contemplating, in terms of a comprehensive ERP refresh, when you can spend $300K on enterprise-scale low-code tied into the system and be able to release new apps every two weeks?

At USF, we've candidly accumulated so much technical debt that we'd have to do it all over again…buy and build anew from scratch. Instead, low-code deployment and integration has allowed us to strip down all these cumbersome, dysfunctional modifications from the ERP system and make what you might call "micro-investments" to enhance student success and operational efficiencies in rolling out user-friendly student-facing apps and workflow solutions for faculty and staff. This enhanced functionality has come at just a fraction of the $10 million to $20 million total cost for a massive ERP overhaul, which certainly appeals to the C-suite at the university.

In the end, digital transformation is all about incremental change. It's about incremental improvement to your current non-digital processes. What low-code allows you to do very well—as opposed to traditional programming and specifically large-scale modification of the ERP—is to transform tactically, swiftly, and at low relative cost. Digital transformation is not a big bang; it's positive incremental changes to how people work, and, specifically, how apps are transforming their work practices.

And we're also seeing virtuous cycles develop. We're changing the culture here at USF. Our clients are working with low-code teams, and in turn, they've started to transform their own practices. Why? Because they understand the cost of failure is low, and they also know there's a huge low-cost opportunity in front of them for being able to deliver solutions for immediate needs in a faster and robust manner. We're not just changing technology—we are changing the culture of expectation of how quickly you can do something differently, and how rapid-coding applications built on low-code platforms can service the way people work.

Notably, there's an additional ROI from low-code deployment on the university campus—the development of a growing workforce of student and staff low-code practitioners. We offer a "Low-Code Skills Workshop" to undergraduate and graduate students, as well as to USF employees at no cost. The workshops provide several weeks of immersion in the technical aspects of low-code platforms and the methodology of low-code app development. Students split into teams to build new IT applications on the platform. And it's been a terrific success.

In today's market, with traditional developer skills both costly and scarce, we've been able to develop a growing, capable resource from within. We still need to hire, albeit a smaller number, of highly-skilled programmers and developers for specified roles. And, with the overall cost-savings gained from low-code deployment, we are able to remain competitive with the private sector when it comes to salaries for hiring into specific, highly-sought-after roles, such as enterprise architects, cloud architects, and other preferred candidates for high-level programming tasks. Highly-skilled people are critical for success. They are enablers. You need them for critical ERP functionality, particularly when it comes to an integration layer that allows for the ERPs to talk to low-code.

Since we need fewer highly skilled people, we can invest more dollars towards a single position versus trying to maintain five of them. As a university, we can't compete on salary against the Googles of the world, or for that matter against local private companies. So for us it's about tapping into our student body for those who are looking for job opportunities and experience. That model allows for us to train the next generation of developers, whether they chose to continue to stay in the low-code realm or move up into senior Java architect roles and the like. This is how you make it viable for an IT organization within a university to compete for talent and optimize the mix of critical, highly-skilled positions with large numbers of low-code developers.

In the long run, one of the potentially overlooked, sustained ROI's from low-code is that we can hire increasing numbers of home-grown low-code student developers right here on campus. We can easily bring on our bootcamp-trained students due to how low-code architecture works. We'll train the next generation of developers, right here on campus, and they can go onto exciting careers in IT, if they are inspired to do so. It's worth noting that our top student developers are actually marketing majors!

The university setting is quite favorable for low-code proliferation. Students will adopt things much faster... and they will code, with fresh new use-cases, solutions for themselves whether they are undergrads, researchers or clinicians that teach. For the low-code value proposition to truly take hold on campus, however, you also need senior management that is willing to take a chance. But CIOs are generally skeptical. They ask: Can you take a low-code platform across the entire use-case scenario? Or, wouldn't it be easier to transform the entire university by outsourcing an ERP overhaul at a cost of up to $60 million? Better to have people in the trenches—from both the IT and client sides—willing to make digital transformation happen with low-code. To be sure, we lost half of our IT team when we introduced low-code. They didn't get it. They didn't understand that it wasn't necessary to touch every widget.

Looking ahead, though, we expect low-code to start going viral soon. This will happen as more and more people realize they have to think beyond the ERP and custom applications to create solutions. We believe the push will come from the business side, and IT will have to react for governance and security reasons. We would love for more universities to do what we are doing and to collaborate and share ideas among respective teams. Low-code can be an amazing connector—an orchestrator of so many workflows and processes on campus via APIs. And this orchestration can become the new normal at universities across the country.

University CIOs and C-Suite execs overall eventually will see the value of reducing technical debt as fast as possible. Indeed, they will question sending tons of developers to do things that yield zero value to the client. You don't want to pay millions in debt before you do necessary upgrades. You certainly don't want to have to chuck the entire ERP or laboriously dismantle numerous apps one app at a time. That adds up to millions in expense dollars that most universities don't have. People are finally starting to realize that ERPs have never been able to deliver on the demands being placed on them. The problem is the cost of these unrealistic expectations is huge in terms of the technical debt standing in the way of progress for student success and overall campus operations.

Future Challenges: Making Sure the Culture Keeps Pace with the Tech

The chief pain point in adapting a low-code platform in academic settings comes down to a mind-set change. In particular, your team of developers should be willing to move forward with the times and take advantage of low-code adoption for the good of the university. The alternative is to remain burdened with old-school, piecemeal ERP modifications and bolt-on approaches. But the willingness to change takes a certain kind of forward-looking, somewhat altruistic (for the good of the university, if not necessarily good for me) mind-set. Some highly-skilled programmers and architects may bolt for higher-paying roles in the private sector. In other words, CIOs and their direct reports must be able to balance the mix of talent required to power the integration of low-code platforms.

That said, the client side can also present it's share of speed bumps. Some clients, for example, are still going to operate on slower, old-school timeframes—expecting solutions to be delivered over longer, extended timelines. But this is the opposite of the rapid-fire deliverables from low-code teams that partner with a business unit in the first place. The truth is, there is little time to waste. Some clients will need to get hip to that fact in the traditionally deliberative campus environment. In the end, though, you need a combination of technology, partnership and realistic expectations to make it all work.

FinTech and the Forces of Change in Financial Services

Chris Skinner, FinTech Expert

We live in a world where young FinTech start-ups are forcing traditional banks to move faster and deliver better customer experiences. This new world demands a completely different business model from financial institutions. There are seven new ways in which finance delivered by technology is changing the game.

ABOUT THE AUTHOR:

Chris Skinner is known as one of the most influential people in technology, and as an independent commentator on the financial markets and fintech through his blog, the Finanser.com. Mr. Skinner has been an advisor to the United Nations, the White House, the World Bank and the World Economic Forum, and is a visiting lecturer with Cambridge University as well as a TEDx speaker.

I am a technologist and have spent all of my career looking at how technology might change the future of finance and financial services. When looking to the future, it is determined by four forces of change: political, economic, social and technological.

For me, technology is the core driver of change, but this does not belittle the others. All of them impact financial markets and businesses equally, and I am sure we can all agree that these changes have become particularly frenetic in the last decade. This is partly inspired by the global financial crisis, but equally enabled by the technology structures that we have today.

Take Cloud Computing, Artificial Intelligence (AI), the mobile phone network and Open Banking, which incorporates application program interfaces (APIs), which, in turn, provide plug-and-play code that can be taken and dropped from any provider to any other service that you want to use. These technologies have transformed the landscape of the world in the last decade, and are now greatly changing banking as finance and technology become integrated. Today, we call this FinTech. FinTech has grown from nothing to a market that received $111.8 billion of investment in start-up firms in 2018.

The first time that I encountered FinTech was over a decade ago at a meeting in London, during which someone had the idea of launching a business that they called "an eBay for money." Their idea was that you could have people who have money connected to people that need money through a platform and an algorithm. That company was Zopa.

Over the past 15 years, Zopa has done pretty well in the United Kingdom, as have many other peer-to-peer lenders and FinTech start-ups. For example, 36 per cent of all new personal loans were originated by FinTech companies in the United States in 2017, according to Bloomberg, compared to just 1 per cent in 2010. That is the reason why the integration of finance and technology is such a hot market space.

According to KPMG, the $111.8 billion that was invested in FinTech companies globally in 2018 was more than double the amount of the year before. That covers peer-to-peer payments and lending, as well as everything to do with roboadvice through to AI, through to cryptocurrencies, and through to blockchain distributed ledger technology. There are thousands of things happening in each of these areas. Faced with these changes, I claim that the business model of the banking industry is completely broken.

The business model of banking is designed for the physical distribution of paper in a localized network through buildings and humans. Technology was then implemented to cement that structure in place. Now, we need to rip that structure apart because what we are dealing with today is the digital distribution of data through software and servers on a global network. The latter is a radically different business model for any business, but is now particularly relevant for financial services due to the rise of Open Banking.

The financial services industry has not been impacted much by this change so far, when compared with the changes we have seen in entertainment, consumption, media, books and other markets. This is purely because it has taken a long time to get to where we are. In fact, it is only in the last decade that it has really started to hit the road. You can see it hit the road in the valuations, vision and rapid expansion of companies like PayPal, which is one of the oldest FinTech firms around. The same goes for Ant Financial, which makes up a case study in the last third of my book, *Digital Human.*

If I had to pick one standout start-up, it would be Stripe. Stripe is my favorite FinTech start-up and is also one of the biggest FinTech unicorns (the industry term for technology start-ups that have achieved pre-Initial Public Offering valuations of $1 billion or more). If you don't know what Stripe does, it was launched in 2011 with seven lines of code that enable a merchant to set up checkout online fast and easy. It's plug-and-play code. An API. That is why the Ubers, Airbnbs and Indiegogos of this world are all using Stripe because it is incredibly easy to just drop that code in and then you can take and make payments. It is so simple that after five years, in October 2016, the firm had a $9.2 billion valuation, with just 400 members of staff.

Another reason why it is one of my favorite FinTech start-ups is that it was started by Patrick and John Collison, two brothers from Ireland. When they launched the idea for this business back in 2010, they were just 19 and 21 years old. And here is a key point about how the world has changed with digitalization: FinTech has created an equal relationship where almost anyone of any age can launch a financial service system.

For example, Vitalik Buterin, the developer who founded Ethereum, was 19 years old when he started that company. Ethereum provides distributed ledger services, also called "smart contracts on blockchains." The vision behind *Ethereum* was discussed in depth in my book, *ValueWeb,* and offers the potential to become the backbone of how corporations, governments and businesses run their next-generation infrastructures. In other words, Buterin's code might become the backbone of our world tomorrow and be as fundamental as the creation of the internet itself.

That is how fundamental this is. Kids who can code are dramatically changing the financial markets, but they don't understand the financial markets. They don't understand why banks are regulated the way they are. They don't understand how banks got to where they are. This is why I see FinTech as a parent–child relationship. The Fin needs to act as the parent, mentoring and nurturing the child, which is the Tech. That is exactly what is happening today. A lot of banks are starting to collaborate and work with the FinTech start-up community, including the Stripes of this world.

However, the most telling figures here are when you analyze the changes in the big banks. For example, I often quote Stripe's $9.2 billion valuation from October 2016 to show how new firms providing platforms for digital connectivity are smashing old firms' infrastructure for providing finance through physical connectivity.

Figure 1.1 Comparison of figures for market capitalization from October 2016

FIRM	ESTABLISHED	EMPLOYEES	MKT CAP
JPMorganChase	1799	235,000	$245B
PayPal	1999	13,000	$48B
Deutsche Bank	1870	101,000	$17B
蚂蚁金服 ANT FINANCIAL	2015	5,000	$60B
stripe	2011	400	$9.2B
BARCLAYS	1692	130,000	$30B

Comparing Stripe and Barclays Bank, you can see that the average Stripe employee generated a hundred times more value, by market capitalization, than a Barclays employee.

Two years later, Stripe's valuation was at $20 billion. That is a doubling of value in two years. Barclays is more interesting, however. The figures went from 130,000 people generating $240,000 of value per person to 83,500 employees generating $480,000 of value per person.

FIRM	ESTABLISHED	EMPLOYEES	MKT CAP
JPMorganChase ⚙	1799	256,000	$385B
PayPal	1999	18,700	$105B
▯ Deutsche Bank	1870	97,500	$21B
蚂蚁金服 ANT FINANCIAL	2015	7,000	$150B
stripe	2011	1,000	$20B
♣ BARCLAYS	1692	83,500	$40B

When comparing the numbers, Stripe had gone from generating one hundred times more value per person in October 2016 to just over twenty times more value per person two years later. Stripe had not changed. Barclays Bank had. In fact, just in case you missed it, Barclays Bank shed over a third of its workforce and increased its valuation by a third in just two years.

That turnaround is down to some drastic action, not an evolution. It is why we are living in such interesting times, because we are living in a world where FinTech is making banks do what they have always done, but cheaper, faster and better with technology. If banks understand that, then they will partner and collaborate with, invest in, and mentor these thousands of new companies. This is why these start-up firms are getting billions of dollars in investment from such banks so that they can be part of their marketplace, part of their community. In turn, it enables the banks to bring the capabilities of those start-up firms to their customers.

This is a digital revolution of planet Earth, and goes much further than just changing banking, however. In fact, there are seven new ways in which finance delivered by technology is changing the game:

1. **Real time**: We are able to fund, save, spend, invest, transact, trade, borrow and more in time windows identified as relevant to us, not in annualized products offered by institutions. The only reason why products were annual was because it was too difficult to service them more regularly in a physical distribution model with buildings and humans. In a digital distribution model, software, servers and algorithms can offer everything immediately and for as long as you want. Forget a yearly service, let's just borrow for the next few hours.

2. **All the time and everywhere:** The idea of any downtime anytime is unacceptable. If I want it, I want it now, so let me get it now. Whether I am in the Himalayan mountains or in Timbuktu, I want it and I want it now. Any barriers to access will be seen as a reason to switch to another provider.

3. **Seamless:** I don't want to think about money and banking; I want it stitched into the fabric of my lifestyle, and supportive of the way I live. Banking should be invisible, frictionless and seamless. If I need to think about my money, it is purely because my devices are telling me that there is something important to think about. Otherwise, I don't want to know.

4. **Personalized:** If things are happening in my financial world that I should know about, then tell me to my face or, rather, my device. I shouldn't have to be concerned about covering my next mortgage payment by moving funds from my savings unless my savings account is empty. If it is empty, don't tell me "Your savings account is empty." Instead, tell me, "Chris, you have funds arriving next week but your mortgage payment goes

out today. Don't worry about it. I've taken care of it by using a 12-hour loan facility at a cost of $5. If you want to change this, swipe here."

5. **Predictive:** That's kind of illustrated by the point above, but it goes further and deeper than this. With the deep mining of my financial lifestyle data, the bank should be able to predict my financial lifestyle needs. My favorite example of this today is the bank that figures out that I catch the underground every day but always pay day by day rather than buy a season ticket. That is because I do not have the funds for a season ticket. In this instance, the bank texts, "Hey Chris, you could save £1,000 a quarter with a season ticket for £2,500. Swipe here if you want one." Okay, so the bank is wrapping up a personalized offer in a loan but at least it has mined my data, worked out why I cannot buy a season ticket and offered me one based on predictive and personalized contextual information.

6. **For everyone:** Why should anyone be unable to move money between friends and family? Why should banking only be for the rich? Everyone should have the basic human right to send money freely, cheaply and easily to anyone else. This is being delivered by technology services for the unbanked, underbanked and underserved. In fact, the biggest change in our world in the last decade is that digital services *can* reach the unreachable. It is a major transformation to everything in life.

7. **Reaches the unreachable.** Building on the last point, the new world of finance can reach the long tail of customers previously overlooked, and can start doing new things for them. The long tail are kids uneducated in money who now get financial literacy through apps. The long tail is the elderly who are scammed and conned because they are financially vulnerable; they are now

protected through connectivity to those who care about them. The long tail are the addicts, the depressed, the gamblers and the mentally ill, all of whom need help with their financial accounts so that they do not drain them of funds on activities that they are trying to get away from. All of these people are now reachable and capable of being supported rather than overlooked.

This is why we have seen radical change to our world in the last decade and there are many developments of non-traditional finance that are creating inclusive societies and new models of finance. In fact, I would cite five areas of change:

1. **Financial inclusion**: The fact that anyone who can get access to a mobile telephone can now get access to finance is why so many people are getting engaged in trading and transacting. According to the World Bank, 69 per cent of adults—3.8 billion people—now have an account at a bank or mobile money provider, a substantial rise from the mere 51 per cent in 2011, all thanks to the mobile phone and the internet. That is financial inclusion for you. Get a phone, get a credit history, get a bank account. It is more than that though. It is more to do with the fact that the internet and mobile telephone is a cheap way of supporting anyone with a bank account, whether that person has a few cents or a few million. Digital is cheap.

2. **Financial literacy**: Considering finance is the major factor in our lives for comfort and wealth, it is also one of the areas most overlooked in our school years. There are now many firms focused on providing financial literacy for children, using gamification technologies to make it fun and easy.

3. **Financial capability for the financially less-abled**: This builds on financial literacy but is focused specifically on the most

vulnerable financial users, such as financial management for the elderly. If a parent gets dementia, Alzheimer's, Parkinson's or another disease that means they can no longer cope, these apps help their children—if they have them—to look after their finances or, at least, help them to avoid being ripped off by scammers and criminals.

4. **Financial wellness:** Psychologists have found that those who have the worst mental health problems are usually those who have the worst financial health. Multiple studies report people with mental health problems are more likely to be in debt. And those with addictions are most likely to be at issue. A great example of action is how UK challenger banks Monzo and Starling are helping customers to give up gambling by offering a block to prevent their financial accounts accessing anything related to gambling. There are two million people at risk of mental health issues caused by gambling in the United Kingdom, so that is a good thing to be able to do.

5. **Sustainability and responsible banking:** An area that the United Nations (UN) Sustainable Development Goals (SDGs) are leading with the publication of the Principles for Responsible Banking in 2019. Sustainable finance, I think, is best illustrated by Ant Forest. Ant Forest encourages users of Alipay in China, of which there are 800 million, to play a game of growing virtual trees. To grow a tree, the system encourages users to avoid doing things that increase carbon emissions. For instance, if you take a bus to work rather than a taxi, you get points towards planting your virtual tree which, when you get enough points, becomes a real tree in real life. You get more points the more environmentally friendly lifestyle becomes. So if you walk or cycle to work, you save even more than if you take the bus.

In fact, there are 19 changes you can make to your lifestyle to become more eco-friendly, including making online payments, going paperless in the office, using disposable cardboard cutlery instead of plastic cutlery and recycling. You can then claim carbon points for the actions you have performed every day and save them into your Alipay account. These points are used to water and grow your virtual tree in Ant Forest and, when the virtual tree grows tall enough through your constant watering of carbon points, Ant Financial plants a real tree for you. By playing a fun app whilst making payments, 500 million Chinese Alipay users have planted over 100 million real trees in Inner Mongolia and Gansu province that cover nearly 1,000 square kilometers of land. It has been estimated that this will reduce the carbon emissions of China by 5 per cent by the end of 2020.

This is where lessons are learned by looking at new economies that had little or no historical infrastructure. We see this occurring in India, China, across Asia, Africa and South America. These countries started their infrastructure projects in the internet age, and are turbocharging their economies as a result. I personally learned this lesson when I visited Ant Financial in Hangzhou, China, as the company has a mission for mobile financial inclusion and has exported its technologies to local partnerships in Indonesia, the Philippines, Thailand, Pakistan, India and more. This is bringing simple and easy financial services to markets that have historically been ignored by banks.

My favorite example is in India. This really brings home what is happening with technology and financial inclusion. Paytm is a mobile wallet that is used across all of India. It has around 400 million users today whereas, just before demonetization in November 2016, it had about 150 million. Because of demonetization and other moves by the Indian government, the story of inclusion in India has risen dramatically, and much of this is thanks to the mobile payments wallet network.

Vijay Shekhar Sharma is the founder of Paytm. He is also a fan of Jack Ma and Alibaba, and wanted to copy Alibaba and Alipay in India. He went to see Jack Ma and persuaded him to invest in his venture. This is why Alibaba and Ant Financial own a substantial part of Paytm. Core technologies behind Paytm are provided by Ant Financial through Open Banking, open payments and open financial services. Using these technologies has enabled Paytm to both grow and scale very quickly thanks to these cloud-based services. As already mentioned, Ant Financial and Alipay are not just doing this in India, but also with partners in many other countries, from Pakistan to the Philippines to Indonesia, Thailand and South Korea. Ant Financial has gone global.

It is worth noting that Sharma is India's youngest multibillionaire today but he was homeless ten years ago. He had been bankrupted by his business partners and was sleeping on friends' sofas to survive. That is what today's digital network enables—opportunity and inclusion for everyone.

We are living through a revolution of humanity through digitalization with technology. It is a fundamental change to how we think, trade, transact, talk, build relationships and build structures. It demands a completely different business model from financial institutions. They must move faster than they have had to in the past. They must be more nimble, so they can change on a dime. They must constantly adapt to a revolution in-progress. It is incredibly difficult for these institutions to make these changes, especially if their leaders do not understand them and their IT systems don't support them.

A Business-minded CIO's Perspective: Why Low-Code is Indispensable for Transformation

Isaac Sacolick, StarCIO

The digitally-minded CIO must lead their organization away from legacy practices, address technical debt, develop new applications, and establish data and analytics as a core competency. A prime business case for low-code is that most organizations don't have the skills, breadth of tools, and maturity in software development processes to measure up.

ABOUT THE AUTHOR:

Isaac Sacolick is a successful CIO who has led digital transformation, product development, innovation, agile management, and data science programs in multiple organizations. He is President of StarCIO, where he guides organizations on smarter, faster, safer, and innovative transformation programs. Isaac is the best-selling author of the book Driving Digital: The Leader's Guide to Business Transformation Through Technology, writes an award-winning blog called "Social, Agile, and Transformation," shares best practices in "5 minutes with @NYIke," and is a contributing editor at InfoWorld.

Double Productivity via Low-Code

Doubling productivity may be an understatement. Consider the amount of expertise and time required to architect, develop, test, and deploy applications. Then, add in the time to maintain, upgrade, and enhance them. If you're deploying the application to the cloud or data center, there's added investment to configure infrastructure even if many steps can be automated today.

A significant part of the work and expertise required to develop and support applications can be eliminated or accelerated with low-code platforms. And it starts with simplifying the developer's experience. In a low-code platform, the platform provides tools and infrastructure to enable developers to create and enhance applications rapidly. No-code platforms take this one step further by enabling citizen developers with visual development paradigms that require no or very little coding. No-code platforms enable tech-savvy people that may not work in the IT department—but have the subject matter expertise—to develop applications with these simplified development platforms.

Both low-code and no-code platforms offer significant operational advantages by providing technical guardrails and enabling more secure applications that deploy with minimal infrastructure configuration.

These platforms can solve many common use-cases, including application integrations, workflow automations, mobile applications, lightweight customer-facing applications, content management, customer relationship management, data integrations, and data visualizations. Vendors optimize low-code platforms for building a group of use-cases, and the advantages diminish when custom coding is still required when building applications in them.

And there are still many use-cases that require software developers to code applications when they have strategic advantages or specialized requirements. So, CIOs and IT leaders must be involved in selecting low-code platforms, and in ensuring that their teams and stakeholders review when best to apply them.

Why CIOs and IT Leaders Should Invest in Low-Code Platforms

CIOs are not just running the business and data centers anymore. Every organization is looking to develop new products and services, improve the customer and employee experience, and become more data-driven. These drivers require the digitally-minded CIO to lead their organization away from legacy practices, address technical debt, develop applications, and establish data and analytics as a core competency instead.

CIOs also need a different game plan, compared to large technology companies, for building and supporting this charter and delivering business impact. Most organizations don't have the skills, breadth of tools, and maturity in software development processes to measure up.

A CIO's role on the executive team is to lead the organization away from the "disruption cliff," where too many organizations fail to transform themselves fast enough to meet new competitive challenges. Today CIOs have additional responsibilities to ensure employee safety and improve remote working in response to COVID-19 and the new normal. Just putting up a collection of unintegrated SaaS tools or enabling virtual meetings isn't sufficient to enable businesses to survive and thrive over the next few volatile years.

Here's the bottom line. If you're the CIO or an IT leader, then you must act urgently. Otherwise, somebody in your industry is going to find ways to move smarter and faster and leave your team in the dust.

Leveraging Low-Code for Saying "Yes" to More Opportunities

Yes, you'll need full-stack developers, application architects, test automation specialists, and DevOps engineers for strategic applications. Organizations still need innovation in strategic areas and require technical skills to modernize mission-critical applications. But most CIOs struggle with high demand for people and platforms to respond. Business leaders struggle with aligning priorities, leaving CIOs in a difficult position. Does the CIO say "no" to some business stakeholders until technology teams are ready to address their needs? Must organizations only look to buy SaaS solutions that meet only part of the requirements or ones where the expense outweighs the benefits? Additionally, every SaaS solution is another "point solution" that must be evaluated, procured, supported, and integrated with other applications.

The thing is, enterprises need to be a lot more versatile with the tools they're using to improve customer and employee experiences, integrate systems, process data, or deliver analytics on mobile and other emerging devices. Meeting business opportunities and goals are not simply "build or buy" decisions as they were just ten years ago. Back then, it came down to either building everything ourselves or buying an enterprise solution and customizing it beyond recognition.

Consider low-code as door number three.

We are not going to build everything, and we are not going to buy every-thing; we are going to put something in the middle—it's called low-code. We're going to use our highly-skilled architects and developers to figure out the right platforms to solve pressing business needs, and low-code platforms as options to accelerate delivery and enable ongoing enhance-ments. Door number three provides new options to develop new appli-cations, accelerate transition off legacy platforms, or provide a more integrated end-user experience.

The CIO's Strategic Role: Low-Code Advocate

The CIO should be directly involved in the selection of low-code and no-code platforms. These platforms must deliver the types of applica-tions required, meet compliance requirements, and align with the orga-nization's overall technology strategy.

But having a low-code platform in the toolkit is not sufficient. The CIO must also be a strong advocate when it comes to endorsing the low-code platform as a foundation for application initiatives. In other words, the CIO should develop a vision of the "art of the possible," showcasing what experiences are required and how the low-code platform enables the productivity and quality to deliver it. Is this digital transformation, enterprise 2.0, or the future of work? Whatever label the organization decides to use, the CIO must deliver business outcomes beyond the buzzword.

On top of that, business analysts must understand the capabilities of the low-code platform. And developers must learn how to get the most out of it. The key is to adjust the development process and lifecycle to leverage the capabilities enabled by the platform. Finally, the CIO should define where the platform enables self-service capabilities or citizen development, and the types of applications best developed by IT using low-code technologies.

These are all aspects of governing the development and support of low code platforms. IT responsibilities don't disappear in the mix. Instead, the platforms should make implementation easier. For CIOs who fear the sprawl of spreadsheets, SaaS platforms procured by shadow IT, or a messy landscape of siloed applications, perhaps the best solution is to extend governance, best practices, and centers of excellence to initiatives leveraging low-code and no-code platforms.

My Early Low-Code and No-Code Experiences

Many CIOs are aware of the benefits of low-code. But there's a difference between hearing about it and experiencing it. In my own experience as CIO at various companies, there were numerous instances where I could not get sufficient technology capabilities to underserved parts of the business. My development teams were all developing customer-facing applications and platforms, so areas like sales, marketing, finance, and operations didn't have the workflow, integration, and analytics to run smart, efficient departments.

Even though at that time, we were at the early stages of applying Agile methodologies in the enterprise, we needed to consider productivity and quality. We were thinking through how to develop applications rapidly and promote iterative experimentation to get the customer and end-user feedback, without laboriously writing lines of code in Java and .Net.

Candidly, I was looking for ways to cheat: to build applications faster and develop lighter-weight ones. I wanted to break the cycle of complexity where business stakeholders—even with all the right intentions—found ways to write requirements and demand experiences that lead to custom software development. I also wanted to develop applications without getting into the technical minutiae. On top of that, I didn't want to leave behind a mound of technical debt when newer ways of applying technology could leapfrog implementations made just months earlier.

I found the solution—this was before clouds and SaaS—through web-enabled low-code and no-code platforms. I discovered that with some structure, some guidelines, some mentoring and the right selection of tools, stakeholders in underserved areas were able to develop technologies by themselves. We did this with no-code platforms and showed how tech-savvy employees outside of IT (with the right tools, practices, and mentorship) could develop and support applications for their business needs.

We found many low-code opportunities, for example, when we wanted to rapidly develop and easily support an integrated workflow, a mobile application that connected to multiple systems, or operational data integrations. We partnered with low-code and no-code technology providers that, at the time, were more often selling directly to the lines of business rather than the CIO and the IT department. Some of my CIO colleagues labeled this shadow IT, but I knew this was shortsighted. Today, most low-code and no-code solution providers seek to partner with business and digitally-minded CIOs seeking to transform their business and leverage best-in-breed platforms.

Key Considerations When Evaluating Low-Code Platforms

When evaluating the most appropriate low-code offerings for your organization, here are some of the core considerations I would embed into the process.

First, it all begins with the realization that organizations have a significant, inescapable and growing need to deliver easy-to-learn, easy-to-use experiences for people working in the office or remotely. Applications aren't silos and often connect employees with customers, partners, supply-chain providers, and a growing ecosystem of participants. That means low-code and no-code platforms must be sufficiently open with APIs, documentation, and already integrated with mainstream application integration, data, and IFTTT (IF This Then That) platforms.

The platform must drive developer productivity and enable them to deliver reliable, secure, performant, and enhanceable applications easily. For low-code platforms, that means developers must see the benefits in learning and leveraging the platform to supplement their coding in Java, .Net, JavaScript, PHP, Python, or other coding languages. For no-code platforms, the challenge is to enable tech-savvy people working for business teams to develop and support applications without it becoming their day jobs, so to speak.

CIOs must select appropriate proof-of-concepts and pilots to validate where platforms deliver the most value. Another consideration is that both low-code and no-code platforms must also enable the CIO to establish governance around the development, testing, deployment, and ongoing support of applications.

Eight Key Questions for Evaluating a Low-Code Platform

What then should you consider when reviewing low-code and no-code platforms? Consider answering the following eight questions in your review:

1. For what types of applications does the platform enable rapid development? Make sure to understand what's easy, what's a stretch, and what's truly out of scope.

2. Does the technology enable a satisfactory user-experience, or must end-users suffer through a user experience that doesn't work well, say, on mobile?

3. How much of the application can be developed with the platform's visual productivity tools compared to customizing much of the experience, business logic or integration with native code?

4. Does the platform already connect with the integration tools your IT department utilizes, or does it integrate with mainstream integration platforms?

5. Does the developer experience truly improve productivity, and does the expected skill set align well with organizational strategy?

6. Can the platform's hosting options and compliance standards meet your organization's regulatory, compliance, and security requirements?

7. How can the platform's development process and application lifecycle meet the minimal requirements needed to support ongoing enhancements to production applications?

8. Does the platform's cost model work well for the applications you intend to develop?

What it all comes down to is this: When it comes to more sophisticated applications, learning to develop on low-code technologies means that you can address a business need that can't be addressed affordably through traditional approaches to development. Low-code guardrails may also improve quality, provide a better user experience, and have a more secure hosting platform than applications developed with native development languages.

But that doesn't mean developers should not play a role in helping non-expert citizen developers with best practices in building maintainable and supportable applications. Yes, a low-code platform may enable citizen development by SMEs and other business drivers. However, business developers still need guidance on best practices in user-interface design, data architecture, naming conventions, testing, and other design considerations.

Evaluating the Longer-Term Impacts of Low-Code

Many key low-code and no-code platform KPIs are hard to measure. For example, are you getting more best-in-breed capabilities for your dollar, and is developing on the platform going to lower application support risks? Also, will the total cost of operating the platform be significantly less than utilizing mainstream cloud platforms and development languages?

Addressing these considerations calls for the CIO to take a longer-term view and ask several other important questions:

- How easy is it to find the talent that can learn and succeed with the platform?

- Can the organization easily enhance and support the applications, integrations?

- Will ongoing investment in the platform help teams develop reusable capabilities and best practices?

- Does the application's performance meet business needs when there's growth in usage by end-user activity, stored data, integrations, and workflow complexity?

- Is it reasonably easy to knowledge-transfer an application's support, based on its experience, structure, and documentation?

- If you have to migrate the application in the future, how easy will it be, and what are the best migration options?

Don't make the mistake of trying to get answers to these questions without dipping your toes into the water and trying to take an application from proof of concept to pilot. If the application is developed quickly and meets business needs, then move on to running it in production, gaining feedback, and then looking to improve the application iteratively. This approach will allow your IT organization to perform a retrospective on the platform to see how to succeed longer-term with it. Ultimately, low-code and no-code platforms should make developing and supporting technology easier.

Low-Code Journey in the Enterprise

John Rymer, Forrester (Emeritus)

Low-code development, which started as a tactical tool, has evolved into a strategic capability. The COVID-19 pandemic has accelerated that evolution because of the rapid responsive action that low-code enables. But using low-code at the enterprise level demands that certain requirements are met. This chapter identifies the key elements of a low-code enterprise strategy.

ABOUT THE AUTHOR:

John R. Rymer is a former Vice President & Principal Analyst at Forrester Research. He coined the term "low-code platforms" and led Forrester's research on low-code development platforms. He is a leading expert on enterprise application development practices, technologies, and platforms for more than 20 years. Forrester recognized him with its prestigious Bill Bluestein Research Award, and Lowcode.com recognized him as a top influencer in its Low-Code50.

How a Pandemic Accelerated a New Era in Business Technology

When the COVID-19 crisis struck the world in early March 2020, the first casualty was business-as-usual. The crisis disrupted the operations of enterprises of all sizes in both the private and public sectors. In some cases—cruise lines, restaurants, elective medical procedures, and sports leagues come to mind—firms and agencies shut down or severely cut back operations.

The immediate cause of this chaos: workers taking up their duties in home offices to abide by shelter-in-place orders (or policies) designed to protect them from deadly coronavirus spread. Remote work broke business processes, first, by separating people from paper files and closing offices that administered paper-based processes. One municipality simply stopped collecting subscription fees for its parking facilities; the crisis hit during its paper-based annual renewal period.

Adding time, space, and familial distractions to formerly face-to-face decision-making routines caused process delays that customers experienced as lack of service. The same was true for business processes automated with spreadsheets and email. Turns out, spreadsheets and email work when employees work in close proximity. Customers (and agents) of a large North American insurance company experienced these break-downs as long "wait states" for requests and procedures.

But there was more. Those carefully crafted 2020 IT plans and budgets were instantly obsolete. Four urgent new automation priorities muscled to the top of the application backlog.

First, firms needed new automated processes to get up and running again. New apps and tools for remote-employee collaboration were included. Second, firms in all sectors needed brand new tracking and tracing applications. Initially, this need was most urgent in clinical health, government, and other organizations deemed essential. Before long, they quickly became vital for all enterprises as they created plans to bring people back to offices and plants. Third, firms needed new solutions to acquire and allocate equipment, materials, expertise, and people. Again, clinical health and governments were the vanguard, but allocation and management quickly became a problem for most enterprises. And fourth, firms and agencies needed new applications to administer the slew of new programs introduced to respond to the pandemic. These new programs ranged from temporary medical facilities to new testing centers to governmental relief programs such as the Payroll Protection Plan in the United States.

By summer 2020, the lessons of the coronavirus pandemic for enterprise leaders were painfully evident:

- Lesson #1: Enterprises can no longer function without automated business processes. Enterprises and departments with fully automated business processes were resilient to radical disruptions like shelter-at-home orders.

- Lesson #2: Automation must be adaptable with speed and ease. Enterprises have sunk trillions of dollars into automation, but only a portion of that software investment was adaptable during the pandemic. A hospital system relying on Java required a 20-day all-hands-on-deck effort to create a personnel check-in application for its facilities. That's an awfully long time to deliver a basic database application.

During the early, crisis phase of the pandemic, low-code (and digital-process) platforms stood out as fast and adaptable. Firms that already had low-code platforms were able to respond far more effectively than those that didn't. A national health system in Europe started an application to automate citizen health surveying (by volunteers) on a Friday and delivered it the following Monday. A European retailer required just weeks to stand up its own delivery service—for it, an entirely new business function—to supplement the swamped third parties it used.

Low-code platforms provided surprising additional benefits. First, firms with low-code platforms found it easy to expand their licenses to add users and processing capacity. The most difficult part of scaling was adapting budgets and procurement policies to emergency conditions. Vendors generally helped with those issues by relaxing and / or deferring commercial terms.

Second, low-code vendors quickly released mostly free applications and accelerators for problems like tracing and employee health monitoring. That's right, vendors of *platforms for custom development* quickly delivered packaged apps (easily tailorable) and accelerators to customers. Why? Their platforms, through low-code development, allowed these vendors to deliver for customers faster than customers could serve themselves.

Low-Code Started with Tactical Apps, Now Is Largely Strategic

I believe the COVID-19 crisis will be the second "market moment" for low-code development platforms. As the evidence emerges of how well these platforms performed during the crisis phase of the pandemic, more enterprises will not only adopt these platforms but also make them strategic.

The first market moment for low-code platforms sparked the initial wave of enterprise adoption. Coming out of the Great Recession (2008-2011), companies saw new growth opportunities only accessible through new mobile apps and other digital customer experiences. No enterprise had enough coders or mobile specialists to capture this opportunity. Low-code platforms met the need by making the new applications approachable by non-specialists and raising the productivity of developers generally. A market was born and an enterprise journey into a new software-delivery approach began.

The journey for developers working with low-code platforms from tactical apps to all enterprise applications is the subject of this chapter. How should software leaders embracing low-code platforms plot their journeys toward greater and greater value for their enterprises? What are the prerequisites for success? What pitfalls await?

Ravi's low-code journey is typical. Ravi (not his real name) runs a development team in the United Kingdom for a multinational automobile-services firm. His top automation priority is empowering repair technicians to ensure speedy, quality work. Attempts to build technician apps using traditional coding and middleware fell short on delivery speed and reliability. And so Ravi introduced a low-code platform to tackle the challenge.

One of the first apps Ravi's team built: A mobile app that makes it simple for customers to transmit pictures of their vehicles to inform repair processes. Sounds like a minor function, but this app and the process it lives in must be rock solid—they are vital to customer satisfaction. Now Ravi's team is automating other operations processes, including big, complex projects. His developers, who initially saw low-code platforms as a threat to their livelihoods, are now bought in. Here are five reasons why most enterprise application teams adopt low-code just like Ravi's team did:

1. Their primary goal is to deliver business applications more quickly. The declarative development tools and automation of deployment and scaling provided by low-code platforms can slash app-delivery times by as much as 10x. The biggest advances in delivery speed come from teams that apply Agile methods to their low-code projects.

2. They want to use low-code platforms for applications that link independent services, often called "composite applications." The mobile app Ravi's team built integrated email, an image-processing service (accessible via an API), the camera on customer smartphones, and his company's existing repair-management processes. The project wove these services and assets into a process rather than creating them all from scratch.

3. They want to visually configure the low-code platform's features rather than writing (and updating) configuration files and scripts. The result can be better application reliability and security compared to apps built with traditional coding.

4. Many traditional developers at first resist low-code platforms. But many eventually embrace the technology as a way to work better for their businesses—even if they continue to use coding for portions of their work. In Forrester Research's annual world-

wide developer survey, half of developers reported having either adopted or planning to adopt low-code platforms.

5. Development teams that adopt low-code platforms almost always start with modest-sized projects that help automate customer operations and then expand into more and more challenging and mission-critical applications. In Forrester's latest available worldwide developer survey, almost 20% of developers reported using low-code platforms to build "core business applications (e.g. ERP)."

Low-Code for Core and Mission-Critical Enterprise Applications

Good advice for development leaders introducing low-code platforms: Start small, prove the platform's value, and expand as you learn. As Ravi did. Yet low-code development platforms hold even greater potential for enterprises than starter projects demonstrate—as indicated by those 20% or so of software teams in Forrester's survey pushing into Enterprise Resource Planning (ERP)-class applications.

For example:

- One of the European postal systems rebuilt and modernized the applications that automate package routing to its 39 distribution centers.

- An international custom manufacturer of infrastructure equipment built 12 applications to manage in minute detail all orders from inception to delivery, including product definition, supply operations, and worldwide factory allocations and planning: filling a gap between its sales and financial processes.

- A big European utility implemented a new custom payments-management application (to replace a legacy enterprise application) to process payments from new digital payment services, as well as checks and credit cards. Millions of transactions.

In these and dozens of other examples, developers are pushing the capabilities of low-code platforms and their own skills into mission-critical territory. Forrester's developer survey found, for example, that the average low-coder development team employing a low-code platform skews larger than traditional coding teams. And more than a third of these developers report building enterprise-wide applications.

These developers reveal the crucial product, software architecture, skills, and processes required to use low-code platforms to deliver reliable and secure applications that perform under heavy loads.

The Elements of an Enterprise Low-Code Strategy

"A fool with a tool is still a fool," goes the saying. Many software leaders approach low-code strategies as solely a product-selection exercise. There's much more to success than picking the right tool (although picking the right tool helps).

Success with low-code platforms at enterprise scale requires a full strategy. Low-code development platforms spark big changes to everything about business software—development processes, software architectures, software-change frequency, team and organizational structure, and governance. Your strategy's goal: Get the business through these changes quickly and with minimal business disruption, while building a strategy with five elements.

Strategy Element 1: Governance Policies and Implementation

Governance won't make anyone popular—particularly anyone from IT. To businesspeople governance is code for "we can't give you the software you want because [insert reason]…" Yet without sound governance policies, low-code development will almost certainly produce a software mess. The worst case we've seen: 16,000 low-code applications running on an obsolete platform in a large North American insurance firm.

Low-code development governance must balance two competing interests: creativity and control. Software development is a creative-engineering endeavor; governance establishes rules, norms, and constraints. High limits on low-code development activities are a good way to limit risk. However, high limits will crush the high creativity that low-code platforms foster. Low-code development governance is a moving target. As the expertise of your staff, maturity of your delivery processes, and understanding of your platform grow, the risks to revenue, health and safety, and compliance shrink.

Start with restrictive policies but relax some or all of your constraints on low-code development as your people learn. Traditional software development lifecycles (SDLCs) will be ineffective for governing low-code development. Those regimes are designed to control the risks of serial development processes unfolding over many months. Low-code development proceeds much more quickly and iteratively, allowing teams to converge and compress phases in the traditional SDLC.

The five essential policies for low-code governance are:

1. **Who builds apps on the low-code platform?** Professional developers come in many flavors. Which are best suited for—and motivated by—low-code software development in your organization? Senior developers bring advanced knowledge of archi-

tectures and algorithms but may lack knowledge about business processes and data vital to success with low-code platforms. Six Sigmas and other process specialists may be better choices but only with training and support in development. What about business analysts? UI specialists? Testers? System administrators? All have knowledge about software projects and the business that may be useful; people in those roles have all become low-code developers.

Lastly, what role will businesspeople ("citizen developers") play in your strategy? Pairing business experts with developers working on low-code platforms is a low-risk, high impact model. Allowing your spreadsheet jockeys to work on managed platforms is riskier but can expand your software labor force. Defining which of these role-players will work on the low-code platform, and in what capacity, will help ensure the quality of the resulting apps and establish clear responsibility and accountability for individual applications.

2. **How are apps built on the low-code platform?** What development and delivery process will your organization apply to the low-code platform(s) it uses? Low-code platforms naturally lend themselves to Agile methods, continuous integration and delivery (CI/CD), and DevOps practices. Many low-code teams use Scrum, for example. Low-code platforms obviate the need for much of the scripting associated with CI/CD and DevOps but offer the same benefits of automation and platform standardization to speed app creation and delivery. Platforms designed for enterprise duty tend to have more testing and lifecycle-management features than average. "How" also addresses 1) development conventions and 2) application change management. Development conventions promote consistent and maintainable application architectures and designs. Change-management

processes reduce the risk of updates that break apps and introduce unfathomable new user experiences.

3. **Which apps do we build on the low-code platform?** A crucial question when starting a low-code journey: Which application use cases will we build on the new platform? In Forrester's 2019 Business Developer Surveys, the five most popular use cases among developers using low-code platforms are (in priority order): complete customer-facing apps (web and / or mobile), business process and workflow apps, web and / or mobile front-ends only, complete mobile apps, and administrative apps for gathering, tracking, and reporting on data.

   Conservative governance policies focus on process and work-flow automation for internal consumption, internal mobile apps for field personnel, and / or administrative apps to better manage business operations. More mature (and confident) groups take on customer-facing projects that seek to advance their brands.

4. **When do we build apps on the low-code platform?** The "when" refers to the priority of application projects. Because developers can deliver a variety of applications much faster on low-code platforms than they can using code, customers tend to build a lot of apps relatively quickly. Prioritizing the timing and funding of these projects will ensure the most important projects are done first.

   "When" also applies to the priority of updates, improvements, and changes to applications. In a modern software delivery process, change management is more active than traditional maintenance. It is vital to progress from "minimum viable products" to full-featured applications. Lastly, delivery of common services to support application projects, such as single sign-on, data models, and back-office integration links, is subject to priority decisions.

5. **Where in the organization are the apps built?** Which departments and teams in the enterprise will own development on the low-code platform? Most customers begin by allowing just one department – usually either IT or sales – to develop on low-code platforms. Some create a new Center of Excellence (CoE) to own that platform and deliver projects on it for many departments. Enterprises with greater low-code maturity tend to allow many departments to deliver applications.

Strategy Element 2: Organizational Structures and the "Citizen Developer" Opportunity

When a department other than IT owns the enterprise's low-code platform, it is almost always in partnership with IT. Sounds simple, but it's not. Most enterprises are only slowly introducing organizational structures that break central IT's monopoly on software delivery. Low-code platforms hasten this change. Indeed, in Forrester's Developer Survey, the top reason to adopt low-code platforms was "empower employees outside of IT to deliver apps."

Traditionally, a central IT group is responsible for all software delivery, either through its own efforts or in conjunction with implementation partners. Businesspeople submit requirements in written form to development teams, acceptance-test the final product, and gripe about the process and its resulting application. Agile development practices pioneered by coders introduced a small but profound variation to this organizational structure by including business people on software teams.

This organizational innovation is far easier to implement than other new organizational structures enabled by low-code. These include distributing developers into business units with only dotted-line relationships to central IT and empowering businesspeople either to deliver applications entirely on their own or with the help of IT professionals.

Yet, the future is surely some version of central IT providing support to distributed pro- and citizen developers. To reach this future, start with the idea that business units or departments are best equipped to set application priorities and deliver many applications themselves. Low-code platforms support distributed software organizational structures in two major ways:

- **Allow citizen developers to self-serve on managed platforms.** Most of the vendors offer easy, inexpensive access to their platforms for tryouts and ongoing work. The leading platforms add guidance, help, and support to the startup experience, often eliminating the need for training. And users build and deploy all apps on managed platforms, opening opportunities for IT organizations to influence, support, and even control the efforts of citizen developers.

- **Allow IT platform groups to delegate software work to distributed and citizen developers.** The leading platforms provide a range of tools and controls to help IT pros set up identities, roles, and permissions, and provide guardrails to speed application creation, administer platform operations and updates, and troubleshoot performance and reliability issues. An Asian manufacturer and a UK government agency adopted this approach, turning their IT people into advocate-trainers for business people working on low-code platforms.

The goal of the above organizational structures is to empower developers and other role-players in the business units to self-serve on the low-code platform. Thus, both established formal training and guidelines early, but are implementing those plans slowly to avoid the risk of chaos breaking out.

Strategy Element 3: Enterprise Application Architectures

Designing and implementing software architectures for enterprise applications is within central IT's purview—and goes beyond providing platform-engineering support to distributed developers. Enterprise applications demand careful attention to structural design for three reasons: 1) to accommodate large numbers of users with performance, 2) to operate reliably, and 3) to support efficient updates and other changes over time. Applications aren't endowed with these properties simply because developers build them on low-code development platforms. Rather, developers have to bring an architecture to their low-code development.

The four key elements of enterprise architecture for low-code development are:

1. **Data architecture.** Enterprise data architectures are built to grow in size, complexity, and usage while maintaining performance. They support not just one application's requirements, but many. For this reason, low-code data architectures separate master data from operational data.

2. **Modular service designs.** Enterprise applications are structured to allow applications to scale up (and down) and gracefully evolve. They require careful design of modular services to deliver the application's functionality. Modular service designs allow developers to scale, manage, and change discrete functions independently of one another. The alternative is spending months regression testing tightly coupled logic and functional modules to either scale or update the app.

3. **Built-in security.** Developers may start the enterprise's low-code journey by defining identities, roles, and permissions for a single application. Enterprise low-code requires a comprehensive set of identities, roles, and permissions, along with a management process to keep everything up to date. It also requires careful attention to data security as a separate concern from access security.

4. **Layers to preserve flexibility across a big app portfolio.** Lastly, enterprise low-code requires an architecture that recognizes that: 1) only some of the apps running on the low-code platform have the same requirements and 2) most apps will heavily rely on external data and functional services. For example, your core data models should provide reliable foundations for many apps, but some apps will enrich and add data in their own specific add-ons. Your integration volumes and control requirements may be best solved by a separate architectural layer devoted to integration.

Strategy Element 5: A low-Code Platform
that can Meet Enterprise Needs

The last strategy element is the low-code development platform itself. At Forrester, we've been seeing for years developers applying low-code development platforms to enterprise projects. A private research study from 2019 added to this anecdotal evidence formal proof of enterprise low-code use. In the study, 84% of respondents in large enterprises had already adopted low-code platforms. Of that total, about 70% were using low-code platforms to deliver their "highest value applications."

Clearly, of the approximately 100 vendors providing low-code platforms, some are capable of addressing the full spectrum of enterprise needs from tactical to strategic. Which ones? How can IT decision makers recognize the platforms most likely to support all of their application requirements? Look for platforms that provide:

1. Development features and tools for the most common database/transactional and process automation use cases available via Web and mobile interfaces. But go further as well: Look for sophisticated forms, page navigation, and progressive Web apps, as well as deep features in case and content management, native mobile experiences, natural language processing, event-management, and access to machine learning services.

2. Features to organize and automate development processes, including collaboration tools for the various role players working on projects, catalogs of shared services and templates to speed and shape the work of those teams, and full application lifecycle management.

3. Tools to design and analyze application architectures for scalability, security, manageability, and updates. Effective tools for testing.

4. Development experiences designed to empower citizen developers—if they are part of the strategy.

5. Operational-management features to help enterprises ensure they can meet their uptime goals (from no downtime to several hours); data loss goals (from no loss in a failure to an hour or more of data loss); audit requirements (from no audits to continuous audits); and compliance with relevant independent security certifications.

6. Evidence (reference accounts) that the vendor's platform can support expected user and/or transaction loads.

7. Commitment by the vendor (backed by a track record) to implement support for the latest operating system and browser technologies as they emerge.

At this writing, most enterprises had repaired the business-process wreckage of the early COVID-19 crisis and were planning their post-pandemic "next normals." Many will require lots of new automation to streamline and make resilient their operations. Many others will require new software to reinvent themselves.

We expect many enterprises to incorporate low-code development platforms into their post-crisis strategies. They're persuaded by the strong performance customers with these platforms showed in their COVID-19 responses, including the resilience of business processes running on low-code platforms. And mission-critical applications delivered on low-code platforms prove these products are effective for more than department applications. A market moment will result.

People Power: The X-Factor of Digital Transformation

Lisa Heneghan, KPMG

There is a disconnect between the culture of digital transformation that CEOs say they aspire to create and the organizational behavior they actually have. Bridging this gap is critical to driving innovation. Chief Digital Officers must devise a framework for innovation that breaks down silos (technological and cultural), embraces diversity to find and cultivate creativity, and effectively drives change across the organization.

ABOUT THE AUTHOR:
As Chief Digital Officer and a member of the Executive Committee of KPMG, UK, Lisa Heneghan leads the firm's digital and technology practice, which helps large organizations navigate the complex technology, risks, and organizational aspects of business transformation. Heneghan is a seasoned executive with over 25 years of experience. She is also the driving force behind KPMG's own digital transformation. She is a champion of inclusion and diversity in the technology industry and sponsors KPMG's 'IT's her Future,' a program aimed at bridging the gender gap in technology.

The Chief Digital Officer (CDO) exists to drive the transformation road-map for an organization. But they also have a second side to their responsibility, which is to drive standards, consistency, and optimization across the organization. So, they have an important role to help the CIO deliver on his or her enterprise IT strategy. But just as importantly, the CDO's role is to challenge the business and help it transform.

When large organizations launch digital transformation initiatives, the challenge of integrating new technology with existing systems usually gets prioritized as the biggest challenge. But customer expectations are what really drive business transformation. It's also true that being customer-centric isn't just about technology. It's actually about the cultural change required to fundamentally shift how the people in your organization get behind the customer.

Functionally speaking, organizations tend to be silo-driven. But delivering on customer experience requires that you challenge silos to collaborate, drive and understand the value your company delivers against customer expectations. At KPMG, our research shows that the fastest growing and most profitable organizations do the best job of segmenting customers and then tailoring their services based on that segmentation. The biggest challenge, though, is removing the silos that prevent an end-to-end (or connected enterprise) view of the customer.

There's also the challenge of keeping employees engaged, which can make or break a business. In 2017, Microsoft did a study in which over 60% of workers surveyed said they were anxious about the introduction of new technologies. Over half were concerned about the impact of automation on job security. And 49% said they feared the introduction of digital transformation initiatives. Much of this comes down to senior executives educating workers about the benefits of embracing digital trends.

What we're seeing at KPMG, for example, is that CEOs—in the UK, more so than the global average—are realizing the importance of transforming their organization from end-to-end. This kind of mindset makes the transformation mandate that much clearer.

In fact, our CEO survey showed that the overwhelming majority of CEOs in the UK recognize they need to be accountable for driving the connected enterprise. Now, when you get that message from the executive table, it becomes your North Star, which makes people feel that much more empowered to make change happen.

It's also true that in the age of COVID-19, digital transformation is accelerating faster than many of us ever expected. The coronavirus pandemic has elevated the importance of automation well beyond basic and enhanced process automation. The truth is we're entering a new decade of cognitive automation. And the impact of this fast-moving revolution will touch every industry on a variety of levels. This includes everything from strategic planning and compliance, to financial reporting and supply chain management.

Bridging the Diversity Gap

Across industries, we're seeing a lot of activity where organizations are implementing Agile methodology programs, not just for technical implementation, but to fundamentally change the way work gets done.

This is happening across the board, in banking and financial services, government, education, insurance, engineering and more.

But there's a disconnect, a gap between the culture of digital transformation that some CEOs say they aspire to create and the organizational behavior they actually have. Every board, every executive committee, and CEOs everywhere are saying that bridging this gap is absolutely critical to driving innovation.

And, yet, the myth persists that innovation is about smart people going off and creating something in isolation. But an innovation mindset is the opposite of that. It's about driving creativity across the entire organization, testing it and, where appropriate quickly bringing it to market.

The question is, how do you do that in a large organization that's traditionally slow to embrace change? Most organizations invest in innovation within specific functions. But that approach doesn't encourage diversity of thinking and creating. Better to consolidate your investment around an innovation framework that people can access quickly. Critically, in the early stages, this means bringing together people from across your organization to flesh out ideas and determine whether they are feasible.

A Framework for Innovation

From there, you can formally get customers to work with you to test ideas in the market. This is where having an innovation framework comes in. It enables you to drive the innovation process, show business value and measure it. But it's also hard to talk about innovation without considering the role gender diversity plays in the process.

Some researchers, for example, argue diversity can be a competitive advantage in the hiring process. Harvard Business Review recently reported that 67% of job seekers look at workforce diversity when evaluating an offer. Over 60% also evaluate the gender diversity of a potential employer's leadership team when deciding where to work.

So, if it's true the best people prefer to work at companies that value gender diversity, and if it's also true that diversity drives performance, then it's risky for a business to ignore the opportunity cost of excluding women from the digital transformation journey.

Gender parity is a massive issue in the age of digital transformation. For any organization to truly be able to transform and be a digital business, it must be customer-centric. Studies show that customers are becoming more diverse than ever before. So, being truly customer-centric, means embracing diversity of thinking and experience to better understand your customers.

The bad news is that the gender gap still persists at many large privately-held companies. Only 7% of board seats at big companies are held by women. But the most successful organizations prioritize the business value of connecting with the inherent skills and attributes that women offer—the ability to collaborate, build relationships and be open to learning new things. These organizations understand that women actually bring massive natural capability to enabling success in the age of digital transformation.

But I would also argue that it's time to take gender diversity to the next stage. Which means pushing for diversity of thinking to match the diversity of the customers businesses serve. I've personally seen the value of this in the dynamics of our executive committee meetings at KPMG. Women represent more than 30% of our team, which helps to drive a far more effective discussion.

It's hard to talk about diversity without mentioning quotas. Critics say we don't need them. But I believe, actually, we do. I believe this is understood at the executive level. When I look at my colleagues sitting at the executive table, I know that all of us instinctively look for diverse recruitment and promotion because we recognize the business value of it.

It was encouraging to see Goldman Sachs' CEO announce that his organization would only carry out IPOs for companies with at least one woman or person of color on the board. Resistance to that kind of change is driven by fear of the unknown. So, unless you have a diversity policy, there'll always be a reason for not bridging the diversity gap.

Which reminds me of what happened at a dinner party I recently attended. A senior person there from another financial services organization was pontificating about Goldman's diversity policy. He was very vocal about his opposition to it. He said that it couldn't be enforced. He also said he had seen many women promoted wrongly. But this is the kind of rigid mindset some people have around the issue of gender parity, and I genuinely think unfairly so.

Motivating People to Embrace Change

When we think about successful digital transformation, we tend to focus on organizations that are really good at integrating systems and new technologies. But there's also the X-factor of transforming organizational culture. The truth is, you can have the best technology in the world, but unless your organization embraces it, you'll never see the benefits of it. Which is why it's so critical for digital leaders to motivate people to embrace new systems and tools. But that's hard to do without understanding the demographics of your organization.

For example, at KPMG we have something like 19,000 people in the United Kingdom. They average 27 years of age. In contrast, when you look at people in most government departments, they average around 50 years of age. At banks, workers generally average over 40 years of age. So, if you think about the challenge of harnessing people power to drive technology adoption and cultural change in your organization, it probably calls for a set of strategies that align with the demographics of your organization.

KPMG has a program of "digital ninjas." Basically, these are people who are passionate about digital transformation. They understand the digital world, engage with it effectively and embrace what we're trying to do. They also help us drive adoption throughout the rest of the organization. So, it's not just an initiative. It is a movement focused on harnessing the power of our workforce to drive change from within the organization.

But it's also true that not every CIO has a seat at the top table. And not all CIOs have the influence to drive change across the organization outside of IT. Which is why many organizations are creating the position of Chief Digital Officer (CDO). These executives mostly come from the business side of the organization. So, in practical terms, what does that mean for the CIO?

Well, five years ago, CIO's were very wary of the CDO role and worried it would replace them. But that's not the case. The CIO role is actually critical because they, like the CEO, are one of the few people who truly have an enterprise-wide view of the organization. The CIO can bring a great deal of value to the organization with their ability to understand the opportunities and threats represented by technology trends. But it's essential for CIOs to focus less on managing the IT estate and more on actively collaborating and supporting the business and making sure people have the right skills in the right place within the organization.

What about the CIO of the future? He or she will become part of a critical technology network rather than just own technology across an organization. The modern CIO will work with the CDO. And companies will also put in place Chief Technology Officers (CTOs) to drive business transformation. Today, the CDO drives the transformation roadmap. They are responsible for driving standards, consistency, and optimization across the organization. In short, the CDO helps the CIO deliver on his or her enterprise IT strategy.

But, equally, the CDO's role is to challenge the business and help the organization transform. As for the role of the CIO of the future? She is not a sole trader. She should be an enabler of digital transformation and not just an owner of it.

What's Ahead?

Some people believe the next decade will be better than the last. Better opportunities, better technology, a better time for digital transformation. On the flip side, the pessimists fear the future will bring diminished resources and fewer opportunities. But here's the thing: The future happens every day whether we're ready for it or not. The question is: What will we make of it? As we enter a new decade of digital innovation, will we choose to be hopeful? Or will we choose a dystopian vision of what the future of digital transformation will be?

As a CDO, I'm massively excited about the future of digital transformation over the next five to 10 years. I think this is probably the best time to have a career in technology. We've gone through a decade of people trying to get their head around what digital transformation might mean. The uncertainty around cloud technology is vanishing. Cloud is now absolutely accepted. It's now foundational technology for everybody's digital transformation strategy. The technologies that are out there are now much better understood. And so, we've moved into a decade where we can make the most of digital transformation.

We can drive significant change in a far more continual way. That's what's so exciting about the 2020s. It's not about having a two- or three-year transformation program that cost hundreds of millions of pounds.

We now have a mixture of cloud and low-code platforms that gives us the ability to make change happen for the business quickly and consistently.

For me, that's just powerfully exciting. Technologists are suddenly feeling like they're not confined to the back office anymore. They're now valued for their knowledge and abilities. No doubt, the next decade is going to be a fantastic time.

HYPER
AUTOMATION

Speed is the Key in Pandemic Response

Darren Blake, Bexley Health Neighborhood Care

Healthcare providers everywhere are reeling from the gut punch of COVID-19. For decades, providers resisted investing in system upgrades and organizational reform. Those things were hard and costly. For many hospitals and nursing homes, it was easier to simply stand pat. But Bexley Health Neighborhood Care did the opposite of that. The London-based provider rebooted resource management, staffing and care delivery with low-code automation to operate more safely and efficiently in their fight against coronavirus spread.

ABOUT THE AUTHOR:
Darren Blake is the Chief Operating Officer at Bexley Health Neighborhood Care (BHNC). Bexley is part of the South-East London System within the United Kingdom's National Health Service.

It's easy to get hooked on the endless scroll of bad news about the COVID-19 pandemic. But, at some point, we're going to come out on the other side. Which is why UK healthcare provider Bexley Health Neighborhood Care (BHNC) turned to low-code automation to flatten the COVID curve and keep the organization moving forward in the new coronavirus normal.

Healthcare providers everywhere were slammed by the soaring death toll of COVID-19, as it pummeled under-resourced hospitals and nursing homes. The situation is already bleak but will become even more dire for care providers unable to adapt as the outbreak sweeps through vulnerable populations in the UK and elsewhere. Like every other provider, Bexley was in uncharted waters with the pandemic. The challenge was to quickly implement new national guidance and procedures to ensure compliance within the National Health Service (NHS) across the primary care and local health & social care system. But the problem was compounded by disconnected legacy systems and manual paper-based processes.

Mitigating Mayhem with Low-Code Automation

With the help of low-code automation, we were able to quickly streamline compliance with the NHS's COVID-19 Hospital Discharge Service

Requirements. That allowed us to safeguard our frontline healthcare staff, support peer-to-peer assistance and deploy a COVID application in less than a week, all of which helped us to avert the mayhem of a full-blown pandemic crisis.

For context, BHNC serves the London borough of Bexley covering approximately 245,000 people. We oversee 22 general practices essentially offering primary and community care for patients registered against a group of general practices. Organizationally, we wrap around all of these practices to provide at-scale services to local residents via a GP (primary care) hub, a nursing hub, and a recently created COVID-19 hub that we launched with a low-code platform.

We factored automation into our COVID response because we were under enormous pressure to adapt our workflows to the volatility of the pandemic. Remarkably, that decision allowed us to transform BHNC to total digital triage in just a matter of weeks. When you're dealing with an outbreak, you can't just have a patient come in for an appointment without first being triaged to determine if it's safe to see them.

Patients are triaged through the door by staff wearing masks, protective equipment and the like. As a precaution, we've also zoned hot areas of our sites for treating COVID patients. Asymptomatic or non-COVID patients are treated in what we've designated as cold zones.

So, things have changed. In the past, patients could just walk into one of our facilities and sit and wait for assistance. But we've adapted from being that kind of physical one-to-one service to a remote triage approach. Today, the first thing we do is assess the service a patient needs and the best for them to access it. We also look at whether a digital solution (as in a video or telephone consultation) can be used instead of a physical appointment.

Overall, we've aggressively embraced digital care, which represents a major transformation in the patient experience at BHNC. In fact, our general practice has changed massively in terms of how we provide services in the age of COVID. Increasingly, more of our services are being provided through digital platforms.

Gaining Insight into Patient and Staff Availability

Changing human behavior isn't easy, but it's essential to fighting COVID. This is why businesses are mandating customers wear face masks amid spikes in pandemic cases. It's also why organizations everywhere are stepping up efforts to educate employees and customers on the new protocols for safely getting back to work. We're basically witnessing a transformation in the behaviors of patients, staff, and the culture of providers.

It's like a revolution and an evolution happening at the same time. It's all being motivated by a growing sense of urgency to adapt processes and workflows to the new COVID normal. And, yet, many legacy patient systems out there are still heavily dependent on manual processes, paper forms, spreadsheets, etc. In contrast, BHNC was able to standardize operations and align our processes across all of our practices. Which means we can operate safely and more efficiently than ever before.

But there's also the challenge of minimizing the emotional impact of the COVID lockdown. Forget about arguing and debating whether the government acted early enough, fast enough, or efficiently enough to overcome the pandemic threat. Never mind forecasting what the post-COVID future will look like. What really matters now is to get aggressive about automation to take the emotional stress out of dealing with COVID for staff and patients alike.

The question is: how do you do that in a COVID red zone where pandemic-related impacts can devastate first responders, nurses, doctors, and other front-line workers? We've experienced the emotional toll of that firsthand at BHNC. Some of our staff have taken ill. Sadly, some of our GP colleagues have actually died. So, for us, it's impossible to ignore the human side of the pandemic equation.

Getting Through the Care Home Crisis

Which brings us to the universally high casualty rate for COVID patients in care and nursing homes. Care homes have been a weak link in the fight to keep COVID at bay. The truth is, many countries were slow to respond to the threat of COVID, and the consequences have been devastating. Turns out the pandemic is the leading cause of death for male care home residents. It accounts for a third of all deaths and is also the second most-common cause of death for female residents—after dementia and Alzheimer's disease according to the UK's Office of National Statistics.

In the U.K nearly one in three COVID-related deaths (over 13,500 fatalities) have happened in British nursing and residential homes, according to news reports. The same is true in the U.S. where approximately one-third of all COVID deaths have occurred in nursing homes. So, why are care homes struggling with coronavirus spread? Three big reasons top the list:

1. Infections can spread quickly via close contact between residents.

2. Care-givers can unintentionally spread the infection without appropriate protection.

3. Many elderly residents have underlying conditions.

Care homes are a critical part of the safety net for the disabled and elderly. So, we launched a low-code automation pilot to establish a baseline for the digital maturity of our care homes. This enabled us to identify where we would get the fastest impact from digitizing our workflows. As a result, we ended up automating how patients register with a general practice, which allowed us to collect patient information faster and digitally track, audit, and make sure residents are able to get the right care at the right time.

Getting Safely through the Care Home Journey

Getting through the COVID crisis means empowering care homes to adapt. Which is another way of saying automation is key to providing quality care, complying with regulations, optimizing care home resources and staffing levels, and isolating COVID-positive residents.

Empowerment has to happen before you can deliver safe, quality care. But, and it's a huge but, care homes everywhere are struggling to get personal protective equipment and other critical resources for staff. Providers are getting rocked by staff shortages as workers fall ill or are forced to self-isolate. We were able to minimize these problems by digitizing our workflows to boost staffing levels, service quality and efficiency. Today, we're fully remote. And we're planning to get through the pandemic to immunization and a vaccine within the next two years.

For all the ways that technology is transforming the way people shop, bank, and travel, it has yet to make major inroads into how they receive healthcare, according to McKinsey & Company. Based on research from over 30 countries, the adoption of digitally enabled tools for diagnosis, treatment, and management, for example, has been slow. And adoption of electronic medical records (EMR) is still not a part of routine care. In fact, EMR adoption ranges from just 3% to 35% in Europe.

It's also worth noting that the biggest barrier to digital transformation for healthcare providers isn't technical. It's a combination of culture, organizational mindset, and governance. In counterpoint to that, BHNC envisions a future where more of our services will be delivered to patients digitally. Digital technology has already been infused into all of our general practice surgeries. Patient contact, for example, is primarily being handled through video consultation. Before COVID, digital transformation was already in motion at BHNC. The pandemic just accelerated our journey.

In the age of stay-at-home orders and social distancing, millions of the poor and elderly are forced to choose whether to pay for Wi-Fi or pay for food in the coronavirus lockdown. How can we get the most out of digital transformation if we allow this digital exclusion to be normalized? Disparities in existing healthcare will get even worse for people who can't access digital care. Better to blend digital with non-digital solutions, and educate at-risk patients who have been excluded from the digital revolution. Low-code can play a huge role in making that happen.

Adapting to the New COVID Normal

We're just months into a new decade and all eyes are on the coronavirus death toll, plummeting tax revenues, and the grim prospect of local governments slashing funding for hospitals, schools and first responders. Governments everywhere are struggling to meet health criteria for reopening the economy.

Rewind to January. We first started to see cases in China. Then London. At first, it didn't appear to be so serious. But then came some alarming modeling and the situation in Italy escalated fast. Soon after that we knew we were amid a global pandemic. For healthcare providers in the UK, it felt like a tsunami was just over the horizon. The entire National Health Service went into emergency planning mode to deal with the massive number of people that would be coming through our community care homes and hospitals.

At BHNC, we quickly mobilized to respond to the COVID surge. As emergency measures were put into place, we turned to low-code automation to quickly develop an application to track back-office staff and improve our ability to do health checks with staff and see who was available to work. Critically, our low-code applications helped us manage the phased redeployment of people and services to our primary care sites as the crisis escalated. We were able to do that in real time with our low-code platform.

Bridging the Staffing Gap

Speaking of redeploying people and resources, the UK has set a goal of recruiting 30,000 new clinical and non-clinical staff into primary care networks. BHNC responded to that challenge with a quick six-week development project to create a recruitment, on-boarding and training application for our primary care network. From a recruiting standpoint, low-code gives us the capability to track and interact with people across hiring teams, including clinical directors and candidates themselves. Also, because we're building applications on a low-code platform, we can launch new software in weeks not months or years.

The Post-COVID Backlog

The COVID lockdown has made it incredibly complicated for patients to get the care they need for pre-existing and non-COVID conditions. Without an aggressive push for automation, care providers could potentially get overwhelmed by a massive backlog of cases on the other side of the pandemic. Across the NHS, experts estimate that as many as 400,000 cases are already being backlogged per month.

At BHNC, non-COVID related emergency department visits have declined 50 percent. We've experienced a 75 percent reduction in presentations for suspected cancers. Fifty percent less presentations for chest pain. And we're seeing a cohort of people continue to stay home despite needing treatment for non-COVID conditions. To respond to this potential crisis, BHNC is pushing ahead with phase two of our low-code automation strategy.

We expect the projected backlog of elective cases will force providers to come up with innovative ways to meet patient expectations for critical non-COVID cases for heart disease, cancer and other diagnostics. So, BHNC will continue to get aggressive with digital technology to reduce wait times, improve safety and service delivery, and basically help us get the most out of staff and resources.

But as we embrace automation, we'll also link our applications to the clinical systems our practices use. Critically, low-code works with legacy systems, which allows us to pull and push data between our applications and clinical systems across our practices. Having that kind of capability is essential when you have to react fast with systems that otherwise wouldn't be able to talk to each other.

Low-code allows us to track a patient through their care assessment and pull related data from different agencies into a single application and have it all in one place. It's like having a bird's eye view of everything we're doing to meet a patient's health and social care needs across the entire spectrum of care we provide.

Sustaining Momentum for Change

COVID created momentum for healthcare transformation. BHNC wants to create an environment where everyone benefits from the digital revolution. Yes, patients have health needs. But they have social needs as well.

It could be a housing problem. Or an elderly person depressed because they're lonely.

The magic of low-code is that it allows us to track the social needs of BHNC patients and map them to volunteer resources. For example, we recently developed a new digital solution that allows us to manage workflows across a large health and social care network. It's called *Share My Care* and it allows us to track everything we do for patients across six pilot sites.

In another case, we introduced an application program interface (API) to create digital records for residents in our care homes. This gave us the capability to unify resident data in one place and track triage assessments, care delivery and care planning for residents across multiple agencies in all of our care homes. We just didn't have that kind of capability before COVID.

Nobody knows for sure how COVID will play out. But it has forced us to reimagine all of our processes, map them to the care journey and make them safer and more efficient than we ever imagined. It's true that we can't predict the future. But we can't go back to what we had before.

To paraphrase Dr. Martin Luther King Jr.: In the age of COVID, we are confronted with the fierce urgency of change. In this unfolding conundrum of massive disruption, there "is" such a thing as being too late. This is no time for apathy or complacency. This is a time for vigorous transformation.

Digital Innovation is More than a Side Hustle

Rob Galbraith, InsureTech Expert

To be competitive today, insurance providers must transform all aspects of the value chain, from distribution all the way to the back office. The "three A's" of Algorithms, Agility, and Automation will shape the future of competition in the industry. But low-code automation is key to unlocking greater potential from all three and reducing risk in addressing the seven fatal flaws of insurance.

ABOUT THE AUTHOR:

Rob Galbraith has more than 20 years of experience in the financial services industry, including expertise in Property & Casualty insurance (P&C), banking and investment markets. Galbraith is a recognized thought leader on Property and Casualty insurance, a best-selling author and notable insurtech commentator. Also known as "The Most Interesting Man in Insurance" for his thought-provoking commentary, Galbraith is a frequent conference speaker and highly-ranked insurtech influencer. He is on a mission to help organizations everywhere turn innovation from a side-show into a functional discipline.

When you think of digital transformation, you may not think of insurance. But over the next decade, technology will revolutionize the insurance industry more than it has in the past three decades combined.

When I wrote *The End of Insurance As We Know It*, I wanted to help people everywhere understand the magnitude of this change and how to prepare for it and how to stay relevant in this new world. I also wanted to educate technologists, entrepreneurs and others outside of insurance about how the industry is different than many others.

Insurance is a financial instrument and a legal contract all rolled into one. It's highly regulated and built on trust with low-levels of consumer interaction. So, there are many things that make insurance a unique industry. But that doesn't mean it can't be disrupted.

That's where insurtech comes in. Some industry veterans may not like the term: "insurtech." They argue that we've always had technology in the insurance industry. And in some ways that's correct. There's a common misperception that insurance is slow to embrace technology when, in some ways, the opposite is true. Insurance companies, for example, were among the first organizations to adopt large mainframe systems in the '60s and '70s and go beyond manual, paper-based processes with new policy administration systems, claim systems, billing systems, and so forth. So, technology and insurance have a long history together.

And, yet, when you think about companies that have brought new technology into this space over the last 10 years across a variety of use cases throughout the value chain, you tend to think of insurtech—companies that are collaborating with insurers to transform all aspects of the value chain: from distribution all the way to the back office.

What we've seen is that the emerging technologies created by insurtechs are helping insurers to be more agile, nimbler, quicker, and more responsive to customer needs. This transformation matters because insurers need to be a lot more flexible in meeting the needs of today's consumer. One way to do that is through what I call the "three A's" that will shape the future of competition in the industry: algorithms, agility and automation.

Let's start with **algorithms**.

I believe insurers are going to essentially compete on algorithms in the next decade and beyond. They already do this to some extent today, but I think it's going to be even more the case in the future. Insurance, even though it has a long history in some ways, is the perfect product for the digital age because it doesn't require massive investment in physical capital.

For example, think about Tesla building a Gigafactory in the desert of Nevada to compete against Ford and Toyota and Mercedes, and the fact that it doesn't require a global supply chain where you're managing shipments from all over the world and assembly and the like. Now contrast auto manufacturing with insurance, which is in many respects just about bytes on the computer. I don't want to oversimplify it, but it's very much about data. It's about risk-pricing algorithms, underwriting algorithms, fraud detection and more. So, algorithms, first and foremost, are how companies are going to outcompete each other.

The second "A" I want to talk about is **agility**.

Agility needs to be much more individualized and personalized. Everybody has a unique set of exposures, whether you're talking about an individual or a business. Too often, though, insurance has been viewed as a one-size-fits-all type industry. By being agile and having the capability to quickly incorporate new offerings and new value propositions from strategic partners, having this kind of flexibility is going to be more important than ever.

Which brings us to the last "A," **automation**.

Turns out that automation is a huge competitive factor. And with the economic downturn caused by the coronavirus pandemic, there's a strong argument that back-office automation is more important than ever. There are tons of back-office tasks in insurance. It's also worth considering that for every dollar that's spent on premiums, about 30 cents goes to covering expenses. That's about 10x more expensive than the credit card industry, which is highly regulated, has large entities like Visa, MasterCard, issuing banks, and lots of fraud and regulation.

And, yet, these companies are able to operate for exchange fees of about 3%. It's true that insurance is a little bit more complicated than credit cards. But it shouldn't be 10X more expensive. A lot of the problem has to do with the inefficiencies of manual processes and verification.

It's also worth noting that plenty of third parties are involved in insurance contracts—beyond just the agent, the carrier, and the policyholders. So, just trying to bring everybody into the insurance ecosystem is a challenge. In 2020, we've still got people that are taking information in on one screen and typing it into another screen.

And that's just one example of where automation can really drive efficiencies for insurers. Obviously, better efficiency leads to lower premiums and allows carriers to be ever more competitive. This is also where low-code automation platforms come in. These platforms enable the benefits of all three A's that I mentioned earlier. They give business power-users or IT staff the ability to deploy solutions and apps more quickly. They allow users to quickly make changes to improve the customer experience, automate backend tasks, and also implement new products and new rating algorithms and the like.

Low-code enables you to build custom applications faster than the traditional way of coding and testing them. In contrast, traditional application development projects have a lot of costs, a lot of overhead and take a lot more time to complete. The old way of building applications just doesn't move at the speed of today's economy. Research shows that lots of companies have kicked the tires on different automation solutions with one or two high-volume workflows, such as processing documents in a mailroom. But I think there's just a lot of anxiety about scaling up. Are companies worried about how automation will impact the jobs of people who are doing manual work? Are organizations concerned about the challenge of displacing people and redeploying them in the company?

And what about the impact of automation on developers? In a low-code environment, for example, are you going to need fewer developers because the platform gives you automated testing? In other words, the human factor plays a major role in how we react and evolve with the rise of new technologies that give us the ability to automate workflows and drive efficiency.

Nobody wants to necessarily be the first mover when it comes to scaling up low-code automation. But I think those organizations that step up to lead in this space can gain a tremendous competitive advantage. In the insurance industry, you're going to see a lot of fast followers once folks see early adopters bring down their cost structure, offer lower rates and be more competitive. It's about getting that flywheel spinning. Nobody wants to be the first one out of the gate, particularly in insurance, which is a very risk-averse industry.

Speaking of risk, In the past I've said that I'd give insurance carriers a B-minus or less on managing risk. And that's because of what I call **the seven fatal flaws of insurance**:

1. Expensive

2. Confusing

3. Very easy to game the system, so there are lots of checks and balances against fraud

4. A cash drain that takes away from your liquidity

5. Doesn't fully cover every cause of loss

6. Doesn't cover everything that you would want insured

7. Doesn't cover everyone that you would want insured

Technology that improves any one of these seven fatal flaws in a $5 trillion industry would make a pretty good business. It's important to understand that insurance is an economic lubricant. I've talked to folks from all over the world, and what I've learned is that there's no robust insurance market in some countries. This is a drawback to economic development because it discourages risk taking and entrepreneurship.

The truth is exposures are changing faster than ever in the digital economy. In the age of COVID-19, it's more important than ever to be able to respond quickly to threats and expectations, and to be able to offer customers more custom products at a much lower price point. The problem, of course, is that it could cost tons of money to stand up a new system or modify an existing system to cover a new threat.

But it doesn't have to be that way.

With low-code automation, it's much faster—eight to 12 weeks—to deploy a new product or service out to the marketplace. Which means you're talking about deploying a critical business application in weeks or months rather than years. Insurance products haven't really changed very much from decade to decade, so there hasn't been a need for that kind of agility until now.

There's an innovation rule of thumb that says it takes about 10 years to build a new platform and another 10 years for it to catch on. So, when I look at the next decade and which technologies will have the biggest impact on the industry, I think first and foremost of our IT systems as a platform.

What does that mean? In the past, we were in the mainframe world. You had these really big, powerful, very fast and efficient systems. But they only did a few things well, like quick transactional processing. You probably had some large data warehouses for analytical purposes, but these legacy systems tended to have a single purpose. Carriers had, for example, a policy administration system, a billing system, a claims system, and so forth. Typically, these have been on-premises solutions that didn't really talk to other systems, and if they did talk to other systems—internal or third party—the interaction was very limited.

If there was a new system or technology you wanted to work with, the cost of integration was exceedingly high. In today's world, though, we've got application programming interfaces and you can create an API layer and basically kind of open your system in a secure manner to pretty much anybody out there. And the insurtech space is critical to allowing insurers to quickly integrate with third parties and offer innovative solutions. We're especially seeing this happen in developing countries that don't have the burden of legacy technology.

Insurers in these countries are coming up with some very innovative ways to partner with other providers to allow customers to quickly add a coverage—for something like an e-scooter—and calculate the rate behind the scenes, premium, and so on.

So, you can find some pretty cool applications of technology out there, mostly in the specialty or niche space. But I expect that over the next decade, these applications will become more mainstream for companies that don't allow their legacy IT systems to hold them back in a multi-year journey to digital transformation.

Which brings us back to low-code.

Enabling technologies like low-code automation allow you to leverage your legacy system investment. Low-code is also a way to bridge technologies that can help make your organization more agile. It allows you to work at the speed of today's economy without having to wait five years for that full transformation journey to take off.

Companies that embrace enabling technologies like low-code are going to be in a much better position 10 years from now. Additionally, it's also essential to prioritize innovation as a functional discipline rather than a sideshow. What do I mean by that? Think about the core functions within an insurance company.

These include an Actuarial department, Underwriting, Claims, Human Resources and Finance to name a few common examples. These functional areas are critical for operating an insurance company, which is why insurers appear to be pretty similar when you look at their org chart in terms of functional disciplines.

But innovation is the opposite of that. It tends to be all over the map. Some organizations have dedicated innovation teams. In other companies innovation is everyone's responsibility. Sometimes responsibility for innovation is driven down to the department level. At other times you'll find it at the enterprise level. The point is, there's no consistency to where you find responsibility for innovation in large organizations.

Add to that the song and dance that innovation teams often have to do to prove they're adding value to the organization. So, innovation tends to be kind of a sideshow. Nobody asks the claims department to do a song and dance to justify their existence. Nobody expects the underwriting department or the actuaries to do it. Why? Because we intuitively understand the value these functions bring to the table.

So, what's the solution?

Certainly, it's important to have innovation metrics. You should have goals. You should have accountability and trust that your innovation people are adding value to the organization. There's also a strong argument for making innovation a core competency in your company, just like Finance, HR, Underwriting and Claims. Start by tying innovation to business strategy. Too often innovation teams become kind of glorified procurement departments—the front door to the real decision makers who call the shots on major tech investment.

Innovation as a functional discipline needs to be much more integrated than that. These teams can certainly play a vetting role to scope out potential technology investments. Business experts need to be brought into the innovation process much earlier than is typical. Don't make the mistake of segregating the innovation team to do all the thinking-of-the-future work and have everyone else just focus on day-to-day operations.

Make innovation a part of everyone's responsibility. Companies must be able to do due diligence to understand which technologies represent the biggest opportunity. It can't just be about recycled forks in the cafeteria. It is critical to focus innovation on activities that can drive business results.

Ideally, your innovation team should have both offensive and defensive objectives. Defensive innovation means looking for process improvement opportunities. This is about identifying inefficiencies. This is important, but it won't necessarily propel your company to the next level.

In contrast, there's something called a moonshot. These are high-risk activities that may not pay off. But if just one or two pays off, your organization can score in a big way. I call this offensive innovation. But you really have to understand where your organization is going to be successful with this strategy.

It's essential to understand the business roadmap and not just what you're executing on this year in terms of your project portfolio. Look at what's on the horizon one to three years out, or three to five years out. So, by the time you get to 2021 or 2022, you can figure out the unknowns and execute with more confidence. Senior executives should always have a long-term strategy that they validate every six months, and they need to make innovation as a core competency a big part of the conversation.

In retrospect, a lot of companies embarked on the digital transformation journey in the early to mid-2010s. And, quite honestly, a lot has changed since then. Perhaps your company decided to go down a certain path in 2015, and perhaps you went with a large on-premises solution that came with a multi-year implementation.

Fast forward to 2020 and a cloud-based solution probably looks a lot more attractive than it did five years ago. The point is, when you embark on a digital transformation journey—because of the timeline and cost involved—it's easy to get stuck. You can get path dependent with a mindset that says: "I'm halfway through my journey. So, I've got to just suck it up and finish it."

But that's the wrong approach. We live in a world of accelerating change. Change is happening faster and faster all the time. So, when you're on a really long journey like digital transformation, there are going to be twists and turns in the road. It's not a straight shot—not the way you mapped it out at the very beginning. Leaders must build a willingness to take some detours into your processes and budget.

It's imperative to build in some ability to pivot in your digital transformation journey, so that you end up in a much better place than had you not embarked on the journey in the first place.

HYPER
AUTOMATION

A Technology Business Needs Simplicity

Ron Tolido, Capgemini

Simplicity is the secret to delivering digital transformation business value. This chapter discusses dimensions of simplicity across business technology infrastructure, applications, data & analytics, process management, user experience, and collaboration tools.

ABOUT THE AUTHOR:
Ron Tolido is Executive Vice President and Chief Technology Officer at Capgemini Insights & Data. This chapter, which includes contributions from Capgemini colleagues Emma Hunter and Gunnar Menzel, is based on several components of Capgemini's TechnoVision 2020 trend series.

No matter how long you may have already been in IT, the pace at which technology is currently evolving is staggering—clearly further accelerated by the impact of the pandemic. The fleetingness of technology trends is such that what was a disruptive, digital driver just a few years ago could now already be the new legacy.

For that matter, words such as "disruptive" and "digital" just don't seem to shine the way they used to. The business and societal landscapes are so swarmed by black swans that unpredictability and extreme volatility are a given, not something remarkable. Also, digital technology is now intimately entwined with business change, to the extent that "Digital Transformation" has actually become a pleonasm.

As a consequence, we might want to call a business that has achieved symbiosis with technology, simply, a **Technology Business.** With business so intimately infused with technology, the quest for simplicity, however, becomes paramount, notably also in the areas of application development and process management.

Simplicity is indeed key to quickly and effectively creating the next generation of application solutions and services, in the closest proximity of the business. For solution developers, technology augments them in the creation of solutions and services—whether software, analytics, algorithms, AI, "things," or a combination of all of that—at a blistering speed without the need for deep capabilities in areas such as bare metal infrastructure, software engineering and data science.

But simplicity is also needed to handle the surge of data and events, coming from an exploding number of internal and external sources. Simplicity is needed to deal with the broadest variety of technology solutions and delivery paths we have ever seen. Simplicity is needed to deal with the eminently complex, highly interconnected and volatile business models of original economic, political and socio-cultural landscapes.

But above all, it is simplicity that consumers want. As they get used to tweets ruling the world, they expect simple messages, instant action, zero friction (which now has become relevant in a very different way, due to the pandemic), and a continuous flow of safe, exciting and rewarding signature moments.

Let's have a look at the impact of simplicity on the Business Technology landscape, exploring the dimensions of "simple" in IT areas as diverse as infrastructure, applications, data & analytics, process management, user experience, and collaboration tools.

Infrastructure, Where Art Thou?

No other area in technology illustrates the quest for simplicity more than IT infrastructure. The retail-style catalog of available infrastructure services, made popular by Amazon Web Services, is now the benchmark for industry providers and internal IT departments alike. Serverless computing eradicates the very idea of infrastructure services, demonstrating just how imperceptible infrastructure can be.

Yet simplicity brings its own challenges. Specialized suppliers can provide an element of simplicity to an organization, but at the cost of becoming dependent upon them. Being overly dependent on specialized suppliers may be unacceptable to some organizations, but so is the cost of building one's own capabilities. Open industry standards may well be the most effective way to benefit from simplified infrastructure services. From virtual machines and cloud deployment to containers and server-less computing, a multitude of examples exist to simplify and democratize access to powerful and complex resources, without dependence.

Unchain My App

Ah, the app. Still the primary means to deliver information or make something do something for us, but they are certainly starting to move away from center stage—if not looking entirely different than they used to. Bot is the new app. Simple chat systems and voice assistants form a front-end, seamless interaction with the user: never exposing an application service, let alone a complex navigation menu. Powerful No-Code and Low-Code tools enable a Technology Business to quickly build these application services anywhere in the organization, with a Bot and voice assistant cherry-on-top. No app harmed.

Needless to say, the more established applications are still out there—albeit as white elephants, eating too much and delivering little value. There is nothing like the breath of fresh air that comes from a successful application rationalization to highlight the virtues of simplification, which consolidates and de-customizes applications—decommissioning the redundant ones.

To thrive, a Technology Business can only be built on a foundation of tidy, well-organized and secure application services, offering security, privacy, responsibility and ethical balance. An equilibrium between the simple and complex, between the individual and the enterprise.

Well...Hello, Data

If Technology Business is the car, then data becomes the fuel. Coming from many different sources and in various formats, data can make any business moment ignite. Activated data can create magically simple business experiences. An AI algorithm can see right through a fraudulent network of financial transactions, predict supply chain outages, determine the credit risk of a new client in microseconds or anticipate social distancing issues minutes before they actually arise. It can know we are bored before we even know it ourselves. Data becomes understandable, prescriptive and actionable.

Unlimited access to all that oozing data goodness throughout the organization is key for any Technology Businesses. AI to the rescue! It can find the right data, integrate it fluently and keep it all aligned—even if the business isn't centralized itself. As the cliché rightfully states, 'the whole is greater than the sum of its parts'—and this is true provided there is "good" data to begin with. Furthermore, while it is perfectly feasible to have a computer that says, "no", "42" or "tomorrow," such simplicity can only be gained with trust, transparency and a demonstrable understanding of how the data has been used to come up with such a verdict. Data holds the power to ignite, but it needs to be used wisely.

Pretty Fly for a Process Guy

Isn't it ironic? In such a short space of time, Robotic Process Automation (fondly known as RPA) has completely redefined the notion of 'automation', thus proving its own—very efficient—point. Not so long ago, automation was perceived as the use of technology to aid or replace human work. Now "human work" is a seamless interaction of a person with a screen and multiple applications, becoming the all-new target for automation.

RPA is surely a great thing when it brings automation to mundane, repetitive and error-prone tasks—never a place for lively career ambition. But what is next for all the office workers who have been glued (voluntarily or not) to their screens for years, when they are replaced by software? Even more so, consider the potential impact of intelligent process automation and the touchless, "hands-free" processes that bring the same cognitive capabilities we thought were unique to humans—until now. For businesses that increasingly run on processes that take care of themselves, there is a clear need to develop Emotional Intelligence: "Technology Business EQ."

Was That Even an Experience?

We need to admit it, as consumers today we have limited attention spans. We are accustomed to swift, seamless experiences wherever we go and whatever we do. And the less we are exposed to potentially harmful physical activities, the better it seems these days. The ultimate user experience is the pinnacle of technology-enabled simplicity as it wraps itself around us in a cuddly warm blanket, adapting to our expectations, needs, safety requirements and behaviors. It becomes almost psychic in its ability to anticipate what we want and when we want it—whether it be news honed to our interests, or coffee delivered by a drone—right on time.

Bots, voice assistants and software avatars—with the aid of AI—only need a breath (or a thought) to get a job done using technology. But can these 'non-experiences' make life too simple? As we turn to Twitter for our main news source, or Netflix recommendations as our only TV guide, a potential "default bias" is never far away, locking us into a comfortable bubble of *what always has been* and therefore becoming *what will more than likely be* tomorrow. The antidote? A proper dose of serendipity to happily discover in a coincidental and unplanned manner.

In It Together

Unique as we may be, we can only express ourselves when we connect with others. After all, a sound is not a sound unless someone is there to experience it. Technology makes it so much easier to connect, create networks, work collaboratively and co-create. As individuals, consumers, and citizens, we are part of a dense social network—a worldwide pulse that resonates in real-time. Whatever the subject, we effortlessly tap into the collective knowledge and brainpower of ever-evolving communities.

For business, "pluggable" enterprises connect in the blink of an eye, seizing opportunities and adapting to new circumstances as they arise. AI systems jump into the mix, working together with humans (or with other AI systems, or even with both) to create anything from business models and services, to new products, and even art. Connections appear and disappear quickly. Information is seemingly created out of nowhere. The challenge for organizations is to find out what is still real, what deserves trust and what partnerships still mean, from both a business and consumer standpoint. Ultimately, it is about fulfilling the corporate purpose and—we can happily conclude—there won't be a case of 'No Purpose' anytime soon.

Applications Unleashed

Zooming in a bit further on the power of "Simple" in the world of applications, there is one, all-telling rule of thumb: *show me your application services portfolio and I'll tell you about your company*. In a world of digital realities and accelerated virtualization, this is truer than ever. The new reality of Technology Business demands application services to be built and delivered at high speed and in various incarnations, as close to the business as possible. And for sure, these application services no longer resemble applications as we used to know them, with even the very notion of user interfaces rapidly melting away ("Alexa, terminate my

GUI", anyone?). Although Agile methodology working through Minimum Viable Products now seems to be the established norm, the quality of applications needs to be enterprise level, as the trust balance of the organization is always at risk.

The applications portfolio of a thriving Technology Business is much more light-weight, easy to connect to, and built on the shoulders of typical cloud-native qualities. Yet, applying this new applications blueprint is far from straightforward, as existing core systems—coming from a different decade or even decades—are a reality to all but the youngest startups. To unleash the Technology Business applications blueprint, various steps should be considered.

First of all, existing applications need to be simplified, rationalized, consolidated and decommissioned. What may have once been differentiating solutions for organizational growth are now all too often petrified, budget-devouring nuisances. Standard, industry best-practice solutions from the cloud are a quick—though possibly disruptive—way to break the inertia. Loosely coupled layers on top of silo applications are another—through Robotic Process Automation and APIs. In all cases, it needs the dedicated mind of a tidying-up guru to actually get things done.

Existing or newly developed applications can be augmented by adding a touch of "smart" to them. AI services in areas such as vision, speech, language, knowledge, and predictive analytics are routinely available as microservices, so no need for application developers to dive into the possibly alien worlds of deep learning, neural networks, reinforcement learning and computer linguistics. Again, by adding easy-to-use, conversational interfaces, such as voice assistant and Bots, on top of applications services, it makes solutions much more accessible and acceptable to users.

When Code Goes Low...

New applications are rapidly built and released DevOps-style—in quick iterations by joint business and IT teams, leveraging microservices, APIs, software containers, serverless computing, and radically automated, high-productivity "No-Code" and "Low-Code" tools.

When code goes low, business gets on a high! The organization may be blessed with brilliant ideas for killer application services, but it will need to deliver them blazingly fast and with the right quality. Classic software delivery based on manual work, complex programming languages and more mythical man months will only get you so far. It is now easier than ever to construct applications without huge coding efforts. The secret is in powerful, AI-enabled tools that leverage API catalogs, prebuilt templates and automation to the fullest extent. And these tools are so powerful—yet easy to use—that they get the popular vote of both business and IT people.

The unleashed application works in the most fluent, seamless way: seemingly anticipating the intentions of its users almost before they are expressed. It's not a beast to be tamed; it's the silent, reliable engine powering business technology. As simple as that.

Finally

Technology has the power to deliver simplicity, and that is needed now more than ever. And it goes way beyond augmenting the way we develop and deliver applications, AI and processes. It has created voice assistants that seem to know how we feel, "psychic" shopping baskets that anticipate exactly what we want, and unmanned processes that run and self-optimize day and night. It brought us smartphones that unlock when their owners look at them, autonomous vehicles that drive more safely than humans, and business transactions that register themselves.

It even produces press releases, marketing campaigns and passable works of art.

Still, simplicity requires good judgement. If one were to deny complexity and go for oversimplification, shallowness would ensue, making us oblivious to underlying facts, causes, reasons and technology realities. The choices to be made in matters of trust, ethics, responsibility, manageability, and control are taxing—but indispensable.

Finally, simplicity can only come after having dealt with all the complexities that are underneath. A tough call for Technology Business strategists, architects, developers and project managers alike.

An Economic Revolution

Michael Beckley, Appian

Authentic technology revolutions are easy to spot because they are also economic revolutions. Hyperautomation is the practical augmentation of the speed and accuracy of human work with technology in relentless pursuit of a 10x-100x improvement that will unlock entirely new business models and drive economic and social change beyond our current imagining.

ABOUT THE AUTHOR:

Michael Beckley leads Appian's technology vision and oversees customer initiatives worldwide in his role as Chief Technology Officer and Chief Customer Officer. Michael serves on the Industrial Advisory Board for the University of Virginia's Computer Science Department, the Advisory Board of the Center for a New American Security, the Advisory Board of 1843 Capital, and is a Board Member of ContactEngine, a conversational AI software company. He is a founder of Appian.

Future Shock

Hyperautomation may sound like some futuristic tech prediction, some far off requirement that may never come to pass. But sometimes the future is a lot closer than you realize. When the US federal government announced the Paycheck Protection Plan, or PPP, to provide financial support to small businesses during the COVID-19 shut-down, banks had only a few days to build new apps and automations to handle the processing of billions of dollars in loans to millions of applicants. Not surprisingly, many took the expedient approach of using just RPA to automate submitting applications to the government. Others used a full-stack automation approach with low-code apps, no-code API data integration, and RPA. Some, in fact, were able to build new low-code automations in just 24 hours.

When the website couldn't handle the load generated by RPA bots, they shut-down all Bot access. Banks that had taken a hyperautomation approach with low-code were either unaffected or quickly migrated to API submissions or automated human workflows. Meanwhile I got panicked phone calls and emails from consultants supporting banks that taken this hyperautomation approach and relied exclusively on RPA. They wanted to know—how were these banks still in business, still servicing loans? I told them all the same thing: You should never rely exclusively on RPA for mission-critical systems. Augmenting humans with automation is almost always the better answer.

Hyper Hype

It's easy to get caught up in the hype and techno-speak, but authentic technology revolutions are easy to spot because they are also economic revolutions. From the steam engine to the silicon microchip, whenever we succeed in reducing the cost of production by an order of magnitude (10-fold), new business models become possible and the old order is challenged. By two orders of magnitude, 100-fold, and the old order crumbles as economic changes unleash social change. Matt Calkins coined the term "Inverse-Moore's Law," to describe focusing on cutting in half the time and cost required to build applications and automate work every two years. Inspired by Intel CEO Gordon Moore's famous observation that as the number of transistors that could be crammed into a microprocessor doubled every two years, we could expect performance to rise and prices to fall accordingly. Low-cost, high power microprocessors didn't eventually just put computers in every home: they changed how we work, how we play, and how we live.

Hyperautomation is thus best understood as the practical augmentation of the speed and accuracy of human work with technology in relentless pursuit of that 10-fold and 100-fold improvement that will unlock entirely new business models and drive economic and social change beyond our current imagining. Driven by the COVID crisis, we have already seen dramatic changes in the patterns, methods, and tools of how we work in a modern society. These changes will only accelerate in the decade to come to the point where, by 2030, one can expect that the offices we left behind in March 2020 will look as anachronistic as telephones, rolodexes, and legal pads.

When we founded our software company in 1999, I was obsessed with finding these 10x and 100x opportunities and viewing the world through this lens. I wanted to help build a world of creators, not just consumers of technology. But I wasn't just thinking about software. At the time, I wrote an analysis of the US Space Program and the "Space Launch Initiative" (SLI) that suggested a NASA-built hypersonic space plane would be more reusable than the Space Shuttle and finally open up access to space travel for everyone. My observation at the time was I'd heard this script before: that NASA promised us in 1980 that the Space Shuttle would fly 100 times per year or more, cut the price-per-pound to orbit by a factor of ten, and soon we'd all be vacationing on Mars. Of course, it was not to be.

The Space Shuttle was, in many ways, a technology and political triumph. But the program, for all its accomplishments, was ultimately a human tragedy with two fatal mission failures. But behind all that, the Space Shuttle was an economic failure on its own terms. Congress lost sight of the program's goals. As the Shuttle program morphed into congressionally-mandated jobs programs spread across the country in a tangled web of inefficiencies with billions in cost-overruns, the original price-per-pound objective that justified building a reusable spaceship in the first place, was entirely forgotten. Instead, much like some other massive private and public sector-digital transformation initiatives, the Shuttle had to keep flying for national pride and because it had grown too big to fail. Enter Elon Musk and SpaceX, which maintains NASA's original vision rooted in the price-per-pound objective.

Why are you looking for hyperautomation? Never forget your goal. Measure it, hold yourself accountable to it, always.

Pathways to Success

While there are an infinite number of ways to fail, the experts in this book have outlined the paths to success with hyperautomation. They have shown you the way, with lessons and case studies that cover everything from how to use low-code to how to build strong and diverse teams to sustain "the momentum for change," all while becoming a better leader. As a leader, it's your responsibility to set lofty goals and then assign clear, measurable, non-subjective milestones to your team. Unless you work at SpaceX, BlueOrigin, or NASA, you probably don't need to lower the price-per-pound to orbit, but if you want to radically improve customer experience, you're going to have to find your own 10x and 100x goals.

In addition to the case studies and suggestions already discussed in these pages, one easy place to start that comes up frequently with CIOs I speak with is paper. Decades-old promises of the paperless office left us with a legacy of millions of PDFs, spreadsheets, Word docs, and error-prone OCR workflows. Organizations are still drowning in paper — even if it is digital paper, it's still a mass of unstructured data that can't be easily worked on.

Just scanning these documents with OCR is a $12 billion dollar business if we only count the software licence costs. Add in the wasted human time and effort setting up or finding and fixing errors every time an invoice or insurance claim form changes at one of your thousands of vendors or suppliers, or trying to create and train new OCR templates, and you easily get to $100 billion—just to start your work.

Start by measuring your hyperautomation project like your economic goal, in this case it's probably your price-per-page—and not just the software license costs, the human costs, the errors, the lost time and productivity. If you have to update 200,000 legacy contracts with new LIBOR rates and each contract is between 80 and 180 pages, your price per page is the time it takes your lawyers and law clerks to process and validate about 26,000,000 pages with whatever OCR and workflow technology you have. If an error takes ten minutes for a human to locate and correct, each percentage point of error you can reduce is likely to save you at least $4 million—and that's with some very conservative math.

A hyperautomation approach to this problem uses no-code integration where available and RPA where it is not in order to marshall the documents from different sources into a modern workflow, where the most efficient technology is used at each step of the process. Documents are classified if necessary by AI, known document structures automatically extracted, while AI algorithms for natural language processing and image processing "read" the document 10x or even 100x faster and more accurately than traditional OCR ever could. When the AI fails, humans don't have to hunt for the errors: the system automatically delivers the suspect field and document to a human for validation or correction—and the system learns from each of these interactions to improve over time. The result is augmented human decision making and work, and much more rewarding, higher value work at that, supervising an orchestra of digital workers. And a price-per-page that should fall 10x to start and continuously improve from there.

The Case for Platforms

Hyperautomation can be achieved in many different ways but this book advocates a platform approach. A high-performing team can custom build many of the elements of hyperautomation, leveraging open source tools, and achieve remarkable results—sometimes even with great speed. But there are three principal reasons why the platform approach to hyperautomation is winning: the scarcity of skilled computer scientists, the need and benefits of future-proofing your hyperautomation investments, and third, the need for resilience in your systems and processes as demonstrated by crises like COVID-19.

The scarcity of skilled programmers and computer scientists is a problem that the market is correcting for, but not in the traditional manner. In the past, demand for labor might drive up wages enough to induce a generation to learn and enter a new profession, as in the great industrial revolution when farm workers migrated to the cities to learn machines and work in factories. In more recent times, technology itself combined with a new international trade order, making it possible for the first time to open up a global labor market and outsource digital transformation to other countries.

Even so, the US and the world were never graduating enough talent to meet the needs of a rapidly changing world, one where nearly every company and organization in every industry faces the reality and necessity of building more applications and automations. Perhaps 10x or 100x more than ever before. And now COVID-19 has only exacerbated geopolitical tensions in ways not seen since the Cold War. Those overseas developers graduating each year are depending on where you are located and what trade tensions are brewing this week, perhaps rendering them no longer even available to you. And even if you manage to employ them, they may soon have powerful incentives, sometimes involving government actors, pressuring them to compromise your data and intellectual property, if they don't already.

This is the fundamental case for a low-code platform approach to building strategic apps and automations. Get 10x to 20x the productivity from the skilled developers you have while opening up your teams to hire legions of non-traditional developers from non-traditional backgrounds like mechanical engineers, music majors, and even political scientists like myself, as well as leverage citizen developers where it makes sense. A platform approach to hyperautomation insulates you from today's skills shortages and provides AI-assisted DevSecOps to protect you from your least experienced or most malicious developer—inside or outside your organization.

Building your hyperautomation program around low-code automation platforms can future-proof your technology investment by limiting the amount of tech debt your team is taking on with each new app and automation. Low-code platforms eliminate and abstract much of the code that would otherwise be required by interpreting a designer's intent and rendering it in the platform. Future-proof platforms encourage developers to stay inside the platform for most designs and only write traditional code as integrations or plug-ins through well-defined and secured entry points to the platform.

Each new generational upgrade of the platform should be able to easily upgrade apps and automations without costly delays to refactor or rewrite your apps. For example, if the platform upgrades the user experience with a new Javascript framework, every app built with it should get more elegant, engaging, accessible, render faster, and work on modern devices with the latest browsers and operating systems. We live in a world where iOS and Android upgrade each other each year and basic deployment infrastructure is being revolutionized with containerization and AI. Every stage in the software development cycle is being enhanced, and the viable business cases for open source and custom code vs. future-proof platform development are narrowing.

Hyperautomation platforms are likely to diverge on the degree of future-proofing they will offer, as some will favor full developer flexibility to write custom code in any language and bury it deep into an application. Platforms that evolved from the rapid-developer tool background and are marketed and sold primarily to developers are particularly vulnerable to creating this type of hidden tech debt. You can go fast with a platform like this, but eventually you may find many of your applications too costly to evolve or upgrade and the sustainability of your hyperautomation gains may suffer. Applying a weighty best-practices governance framework can help, but can also slow down projects with extra review cycles—contrary to the entire hyperautomation mission.

Stand-alone RPA products are perhaps the worst offenders when it comes to future-proofing your hyperautomation investment. Bots are great when APIs aren't available and speed is of the essence, AND systems are stable. But introduce change and variation in workload, networks, and systems, and Bot error rates will creep up. RPA vendors have recently responded to their failure to scale the vast majority of projects beyond 50 Bots by bolting on a variety of quick fixes (monitoring tools, notifying humans when Bots break), but they don't address the fundamental problem that Bots aren't best for everything and the more Bots you pile on your legacy environment, the more brittle and failure-prone your digital workforce can become.

Your Journey Starts Now

Hyperautomation calls for a holistic approach from the start to achieve a future-proof model of augmenting, not replacing, human strategic thinking and work. Model your end-to-end process with humans in charge and augment them with RPA Bots and other automation technologies like AI, business rules, and API integrations for maximum efficiency. Use low-code if you need a new app, add automation or start with automation if the priority is working with data in existing apps. But monitor, optimize, repurpose, and retire legacy systems and legacy digital workers (Bots or algorithms) as circumstances evolve. If you keep to these fundamentals, your hyperautomation goal of 10x and 100x improvement is within your reach.

HYPERAUTOMATION